DO NOT REMOVE
CARDS FROM POCKET

COPING WITH

Weapons and Violence in Your School and on Your Streets

Maryann Miller

THE ROSEN PUBLISHING GROUP, INC./NEW YORK

Maryann Miller is a journalist and freelance writer who has written for *Lady's Circle, Byline, Sunday Woman, Marriage and Family Living,* and *Plano Magazine.* At *Plano Magazine* she served as editor from 1983 to 1986. She is currently a Public Relations Consultant for The Catholic Foundation, the largest Catholic endowment institution in Texas.

Her educational background is in sociology and psychology, and she has continued those interests by volunteering in social programs through her church.

Ms. Miller has been married for over twenty-six years, has five children and three grandchildren.

Published in 1993 by The Rosen Publishing Group, Inc.
29 East 21st Street, New York, NY 10010

Copyright 1993 by Maryann Miller

First Edition

Library of Congress Cataloging-in-Publication

Miller, Maryann.
    Coping with weapons and violence in your school and on your streets / Maryann Miller.—1st ed.
      p.   cm.
    Includes bibliographical references and index
    ISBN 0-8239-1435-6
    1. Juvenile delinquency—United States. 2. Gangs—United States. 3. Violent Crimes—United States. 4. School violence—United States. I. Title.
HV9104.M55 1993
364.3'6'0973—dc20
                                     92-42611
                                         CIP

Contents

Introduction

Violence is something most of us hope we will never be a part of, certainly not as a victim. Yet, as repulsive as violence is, we all have a macabre attraction to it. We slow down at the scene of an accident. We watch slasher movies. We even watch a fistfight with some weird fascination.

This mixture of repulsion and fascination has puzzled experts since the beginning of time. There's no easy explanation for those reactions. Nor is there an easy explanation for why mankind has a kind of violence so different from other animals.

What is even more puzzling to many people is why violence has increased as civilization has progressed. If the need for violent behavior was based on some instinctive drive for survival and protection, why has it become a daily concern in many of our cities and neighborhoods throughout the country?

Author John Langone considers violence to be our fastest-growing public health problem, and various studies prove that:

- Violence has replaced infection as the leading killer of young people in the U.S.
- Some 23,000 people are murdered in the United States each year—roughly 400 a week, or one every half hour. Most of the victims know their assailant

because the attacks are usually the result of a family or neighborhood argument, a gang war, or a drug-related quarrel. About a third of the victims are killed by total strangers, sometimes for no apparent reason.

• People younger than eighteen commit a quarter of the violent crimes, and they are more likely than adults to do so in gangs of three or more. Moreover, the number of murders committed by young people between the ages of fifteen and twenty-four has more than doubled over the past twenty-five years. Most violent crimes are, in fact, committed by this age group.

• More than 80,000 forcible rapes occur in a year.

• Nearly 25 million households experience a crime of violence or theft in any given year.

• More than 100,000 teachers are physically assaulted by students every year.

• According to the Federal Bureau of Investigation, about 46 percent of all violent crimes reported during 1987 were committed by youths between the ages of ten and twenty-four.

Other studies have shown that violence is increasing and that one in every five people will probably be a victim of violence or crime sometime. Considering the implications of all these statistics, it makes one wonder when and if it will ever change.

Many experts have asked themselves the same question and looked long and hard at the "why" of it all from many angles. Some of the reasons people are violent toward each other are eternal. As John Langone puts it, "So long as human beings hate and love, are greedy and jealous, hungry, poor, and insane, or seek power, they will strike out to injure one another, either physically or emotionally, or even to kill."

Today's violence seems to go far beyond those standard reasons, however. Random acts of violence with no apparent motive are not uncommon, and the brutality of those acts is frightening. This is of great concern to professionals in law enforcement and mental health. It should be equally so to us as individuals, not just because we stand the chance of becoming one of the statistics, but because of what it says about whether we are going forward or backward as a society.

We should be alarmed about our level of tolerance for violence. Most people, even the youngest children, are accustomed to seeing graphic portrayals of violent acts. We see them in the news, in movies and television shows, and sometimes in the street in front of our houses.

On February 26, 1992, two students were shot and killed at Thomas Jefferson High School in Brooklyn, New York. At one boy's funeral, the Reverend Johnny Ray Youngblood said the tragedy went far beyond the deaths of the two boys. "The tragedy is that what used to be unusual is now usual. The twenty-four-hour virus—the all-around-the-clock virus—of violent death threats to young men and women should be unthinkable, but it's commonplace."

In his eulogy, Mr. Youngblood made an impassioned plea for everyone to think. He quoted the Jewish social philosopher Hannah Arendt, who thought that ". . . evil was not demonic, but more the absence of thinking—a kind of blankness, an emptiness."

Repeatedly, he asked people, both young and old, to stop and think. Stop the actions and reactions, and think. Stop courting death, and think. Stop the rhetoric, and think. "If we don't decide to live and to be better than we are, then all that we do is in vain. Today . . . if we don't think some new thoughts about how to revolutionize and turn our community, city, and our country around, I'll be seeing more of you in circumstances like these."

The pain and anguish Mr. Youngblood felt at the unnecessary deaths of two young people is felt across the nation as violence erupts with volcanic force. It must stop before we are all swept away.

Many of you may be facing problems of violence on a personal level. You deal with it at school, in your neighborhood, and maybe even in your home. This book will not change any of that, but my hope is that you will find something in these pages that will help you to understand and to cope.

For those who are not direct victims of violence, this book is for you, too. We all suffer because of the increase of violence in our society, and we desperately need to find a way to turn the tide. A greater understanding of the patterns of violence and human behavior may give you an insight that will be the first step toward effecting a change.

CHAPTER 1

Violence, a Way of Life

Tim is nineteen years old and has just graduated from high school in Dallas, Texas. If things had gone differently, however, Tim probably would not have graduated. There is even a distinct possibility that he would not have been around to tell his story.

As early as third grade, Tim was involved in numerous fistfights. Instead of playing tag during recess, Tim and some others would end up in a brawl. First they would start horsing around. Then someone would be annoyed at something Tim said, and before he could think about it, the fight was on.

Childhood is supposed to be a time of innocence. Eight-year-olds are not supposed to be fighting all the time. They should be playing baseball, or bike riding, or playing video games with their friends. They shouldn't be getting expelled from school for giving someone a bloody nose.

But childhood is not normal for all people.

To fight or not to fight was not much of a choice in Tim's neighborhood, which was primarily low-income black. Fighting was a way of life. "You had to stand up for yourself," Tim says. "Don't let anyone think you were weak or afraid. Then they would really be after you."

The "they" Tim referred to were older kids who roved in gangs looking for younger kids to victimize. Some of them were dopers or dealers, others were just kids who thought they had something to prove. To be accepted and to be left alone in this neighborhood, you had to live by the code. You had to prove you were as tough as they were. So everyone learned early on how to be tough.

When Tim was about to be kicked out of school in third grade, his parents decided to get him out of the neighborhood. He went to live with an older sister and her family and transferred to another school.

Away from the old neighborhood, Tim had less trouble, but he can't really say why. The best answer he can give is that he had less to prove in the new area. He also stayed more to himself, avoiding the other kids and any possibility of trouble.

Within a few years, however, things changed at Tim's sister's house, and he ended up back in the old neighborhood. It was almost as if he had never left. He was fighting all the time, and by eighth grade he was carrying a gun to school. Not that he had to because of a specific threat. It was just part of maintaining his reputation. He still had to be tougher, stronger than the next guy. "Everybody had guns," Tim says. "It's just the way things were."

Tim says it was easy to get a gun. You could just pass the word on the street and one would become available. The prices ranged from $50 to $100, and Tim is sure they were stolen.

Tim kept the gun hidden at home, but one day his younger sister found it. She showed it to their mother, who immediately took it to the police. Since it was a first offense, Tim was given probation.

Did it bother him that his mother turned him in? Tim shrugs. "She didn't like all that stuff going on," he says, pausing for a moment to think, then shrugging again. "She just did what she had to do. I was wrong. I know it."

If this were fiction, this would be the moment when the character turns around, learns his lesson, and never goes back to his old ways. But Tim didn't. He was still controlled too much by the forces from outside and within. The threats were still there, and his natural response was to strike back.

Oddly, Tim was the only member of his family to get involved in serious violence. Trying to come up with a reason, he is at a loss. He can't claim lack of parental support or good role models. His parents are good, hard-working people who tried to teach their children the value of education and doing the right thing.

Most of the time they were not even aware of how Tim behaved away from home. It was as if he had two separate lives. At home, he tried to behave properly out of respect for his parents. His father was strict and expected a lot of the children, but he was reasonable. "He just wanted us to do good and be good," Tim says simply.

Why this influence was not enough to turn him away from the course of violence, Tim has no idea, although he does suggest that it had something to do with his immaturity.

Perhaps there is some insight in that observation. For in fact, Tim says he seldom thought about what he was doing or why. Not the way he has thought about it recently. He just did what it seemed like he had to do, and the first time he was involved in serious violence involving a gun, he was sixteen.

"This older guy, Frank, was hitting on my girlfriend. When she told me about it, I was mad. So I went out to find him. He asked me what I was going to do about it, and pulled out a knife. So I pulled out a gun and put it in his face. Told him if he moved, I'd kill him."

That day Frank backed down, and Tim walked away.

"The next day I was at a park playing basketball and Frank showed up. My brother asked him what he was doing there. Was he trying to fight me? Then Frank started a fight with my brother and I told him to let him go. So Frank started fighting with me. Then I got my gun and told him I was going to leave. He said if I tried to leave, he'd follow me all the way to my house. Then he went to his car and pulled out a two-by-four and started after me. I shot him in the leg."

The police were called, and Tim ended up in jail. Because he was only sixteen, he was put on probation. He was lucky, and he admits that the fear of prison was the only thing that had kept him from being involved in criminal activity before.

In his mind, what he did was not criminal. He knows that the law says it is, but for him it was survival. In fact, when asked if he felt any remorse or regret, he has a mixed response. He says he would not want to kill anyone; the consequences would be too high. But he would have been relieved to put an end to the vendetta between himself and Frank. For several years they skirmished every time they came near each other.

"One time," Tim relates, "we pulled up next to each other at a red light. He started telling me what he was going to do to me, and I started telling him right back. Then he told me to pull over, and he got out of his car with a twelve-gauge shotgun. He put it in front of my windshield. I didn't move. I just sat there, and finally he walked away."

The bad feelings between the two of them carried over into school, where one or the other would start a fight in the halls. Eventually, school officials wanted to expel both of them. It was only through the intervention of Tim's teachers that he was put in a home-study program so he could finish his senior year.

The teachers recognized that expelling Tim would cast him adrift with no hope. "Tim is a very bright boy," said teacher Mona Sizer. 'If he didn't graduate, there's no telling how he would end up. We just thought it was important to give him a chance."

Tim is still an angry young man, with currents that run deep beneath a calm exterior. But he has realized some things about himself, and he has made plans for the future.

Although he has little remorse for what he has done, he has come to an awareness that he has to change some things about himself. If he wants to fit into a broader scope of society not governed by the rules of the "neighborhood," he has to move away from his normal response to others. "I've got to change my attitude," he admits. "Fighting and shooting is not the way [to solve problems]."

Asked if he has learned anything from his experiences, he says, "Yes, I learned that I'm smart. That I can do good in school if I try. That I can do something better for myself."

Tim wants to go to college. He has a good job with a large business doing entry-level clerical work, and he likes it. But he doesn't want to do filing the rest of his life. He'd like to study business administration.

His plan is to apply at a community college next fall with the hope that he can continue until he gets a degree.

He seems very motivated and determined, and much of that comes from his girlfriend, Danielle.

Even though she never liked the violence, Danielle has always stood by him. She has quietly accepted "the way things are" in the neighborhood, understanding that Tim did things because he felt he had to. But she hopes that is all behind them now. She, too, has plans for the future. A home. A family. A normal life.

CHAPTER 2

Webster Says . . . Defining the Problem

There was once a time when school violence was associated with the bully who would knock you down in the playground. He would probably pick on you until you either fought him and won, or found some other way to let him know you wouldn't be a victim anymore.

Today, school violence has come off the playground, and the victims suffer more than just a bloody nose.

In 1991 the Department of Justice issued the results of a six-month study conducted in 1988–89 showing that 2 percent of students twelve to nineteen were victims of violent offenses. The study found that public school students were more likely to be victims than students in private schools, and ninth-grade students were victimized more than students in all higher grades.

Seventy-nine percent of the young people who participated in the study said there were no gangs in their schools. Fifteen percent said there were, and 5 percent were unsure. Sixteen percent reported incidents of a student attacking or threatening a teacher.

Thirty-one percent said that alcohol was easy to obtain at or near school; 47 percent said it was hard or impossible to obtain. In reference to drugs, 30 percent said it was easy to obtain marijuana; 11 percent, cocaine; and 9 percent, crack. Forty-three percent said it was hard or impossible to obtain marijuana; 58 percent, cocaine; and 57 percent, crack.

Close to two percent of the students admitted that they had carried weapons to school to protect themselves. Those weapons included guns, knives, brass knuckles, razor blades, and spiked jewelry.

Many schools in large urban areas now have security systems and metal detectors at every entrance. Security guards patrol the halls, but still the violence goes on. Students, teachers, and administrators live with a growing sense of fear and anxiety as more and more incidents of violence occur.

According to one school psychologist, a small percentage of students are actively looking for trouble. He calls those students the "hunters." Another small percentage are direct victims, and about 90 percent of the kids are just caught in the middle. Because of the actions of the hunters, the great majority of students have to put up with intense security all day long.

Students at one school begin their day by passing through metal detectors. One police officer is on duty full time patrolling the halls. Two more police officers are on duty before and after school when the buses are loading and unloading. In addition to the police officers, seven assistant principals monitor the halls.

Some students welcome the security. It helps them feel safer. One student says, "You wake up every morning and wonder what's going to happen. Is one of your friends going to get shot?"

Another student says, "When you go to school, you're scared because you don't know what's going to happen to you."

But the flip side of school security is that it creates another set of problems.

On a television special titled "Back to School" (February 16, 1992), Paul Rodreguiz discussed the issue of violence at school with a number of students in Los Angeles. They were very frank.

"You come to school to get an education," one student said. "And all this searching makes you feel worse. Like you're locked up in some kind of prison."

This student said he knows the gates are to keep other people out, but it doesn't make him feel any better. "You think you're at school and it's a safe place and this [violence] comes out of nowhere. Sometimes you're even scared to go to school."

The purpose of fear under normal circumstances is to warn us of possible danger. We hear a strange noise and we are suddenly alert and on guard. Physically, we experience a surge of energy and a heightened awareness. That is an integral part of our survival mechanism, and we wouldn't want to be without it.

Too much fear, however, can be counterproductive. It can put us "on guard" all the time, causing extreme nervousness and anxiety. Some people actually get "frozen" in fear, becoming unable to function normally.

The seriousness of the new problems created by school violence cannot be ignored. Beyond the physical danger, it threatens the educational system itself. How can teachers teach or students learn in an atmosphere of fear and anxiety? And how many students drop out because they don't want to deal with it anymore?

Jason is an example. He quit school only a few months into his sophomore year because, "I figured my life would be a whole lot easier if I didn't have to deal with the hassles at school."

The hassles were twofold. A gang of black kids had been terrorizing white kids for several years. Jason vividly recalls an incident in seventh grade when about twenty-five black kids jumped two white kids after a pep rally. "We were all just having fun. Nothing was going on. Then all of a sudden, there they were."

Over the next few years, gang members would threaten and try to provoke Jason into fights. Sometimes they followed him home from school and tried to corner him. Other times they tried to get him to fight in the classroom. "This one kid in particular always wanted to fight," Jason says. "This one day before class started, he was in my face, pushing me to fight. I didn't want to, so I just sat there. Then the teacher walked in and sent us both to the principal.

"The principal was going to send the other guy home and let me go back to class, but I didn't want to. I knew his friends would try to jump me. So I told the principal I wanted to go home, too. And I never went back."

Jason admits that he had had other problems in school. He wasn't a great student. He acted up in class and always managed to be on the wrong side of teachers, but he wouldn't have quit just because of that. "I probably would have stayed in school if it hadn't been for the trouble with the gangs."

Within a year after he quit school, Jason honored a promise to his mother to get his GED. Now he has a good job with a security company, and he hopes to make ~~~~~ thing of himself. But he still feels a sense of injustice about it all.

Jason's story has a happy ending, but what about all those other kids who quit school under similar circumstances? How many of them end up with no future at all?

LOOKING AT IT FROM ANOTHER ANGLE

School violence is not limited to fights between students. Teachers, principals, and other school personnel are becoming targets at a frightening rate. During the fall semester of 1991, one large city recorded forty-seven assaults on teachers, principals, or security guards.

Psychologists attribute the increase in violence to students' inability to respect authority, handle anger, and resolve problems. Students who are burdened with the pressures of poverty, family problems, and difficulty with schoolwork seem to erupt at the slightest prodding by school staff.

Those eruptions are not limited to inner-city schools with a history of gangs and violence. A teacher in an upper middle-class suburb said they deal with violence, too, if on a smaller scale.

Since most of these students don't face the same problems inner-city school kids do, what causes their violence?

That teacher attributed it to lack of respect for authority and lack of accountability, for which she blames the parents. "Those kids are being raised by folks who grew up in the sixties. A lot of them have no respect for authority themselves, so they haven't taught it to their kids."

Katie, a high school senior, agrees that some kids defy authority. But she also cites other reasons, the major one being boredom. "There's nothing to do," she says. "Many kids don't have things they're involved in and they have too much time with nothing to do."

Some of the blame for that can be laid to parents who regularly leave their kids alone after school, not only unsupervised, but without guidance or support system. Kids need the sanctuary of home, where they can find love, security, and help with problems. And often they need someone to talk to right now, not three or four hours later.

Giving parents a break, high school junior Matt thinks some of the blame has to go to the kids themselves. "You don't have to be bored unless you want to," he says. "Everybody can find something to do, and someone to talk to."

Concern for teachers' safety has become a nationwide issue. Legislators in Florida have proposed a law to allow teachers to carry stun guns for self-defense, and the school board of the Houston Independent School District authorized security officers to carry guns in school.

"Something has to be done," says Bob Baker, president of the Classroom Teachers of Dallas Association. "Too many teachers are suffering from the stress of trying to deal with a sense of lawlessness in the schools."

In May 1991, a fourteen-year-old student at a suburban school in Texas brought a gun to school, threatened several students, and fired at an assistant principal. While the principal was meeting with the boy's mother to discuss what action they should take, the boy left the school.

He returned later, his face and stomach painted like a warrior, and confronted the assistant principal outside her office. Pulling a gun, he forced her to back into the room, where the door automatically locked behind him. She radioed for help with a walkie-talkie, then managed to climb out the window. The school was immediately evacuated, but one teacher volunteered to stay. "I knew him. He was one of my students, and I just thought that if I stayed with him and kept him talking, we would have a chance to save him."

There was considerable concern over whether the boy would turn the gun on himself. He had apparently told other students that he wanted to hurt several school administrators and then himself. "I wasn't afraid of him," said the assistant principal, "I just kept thinking about how I could help him. He needs help."

Without doubt, students who try to solve their problems with guns need help, but understanding that changes nothing for the moment. Students and teachers have to be concerned for their own safety.

If you attend a school that has not experienced violence, you may wonder why you should be concerned; it is a problem you won't have to face any time soon. Well, that's what those people in Texas thought. They had had no incidents of violence before, so they had nothing to worry about.

Unfortunately, school violence is a spreading epidemic, and until a cure is found, everyone has to worry. If you should ever find yourself in the middle of a violent situation, there are a few things you can do to protect yourself and perhaps even help prevent a tragedy.

- **Acknowledge the seriousness of the situation**. The first time you are involved in a violent incident, it may have a sense of unreality. Or it may cause a group sense of excitement. But it is definitely no time to get caught up in that excitement. If the gun starts going off, real people are going to get hurt, and one of them could be you.
- **Don't panic**. Yeah, right. Like, what are we sup-

posed to do if some guy is waving a gun around? Stay calm the best way you can. Try taking a few deep breaths to steady yourself, or focus on something else for a moment. Whatever you do to keep from screaming or running could make a world of difference. Any sudden noise or movement could rattle the person with the gun and cause him to start shooting.

- **Follow orders**. Police and school officials will have no time for explanations and reasons. They'll probably be yelling orders at you, and they'll need you to do what they say immediately.
- **Blow the whistle if you have to**. If a kid at your school ever confides in you that he is considering violence, tell someone. Maybe that incident in Texas could have been averted had one of the other students spoken up. It's easier to prevent a dangerous situation than to survive one.

OTHER TYPES OF VIOLENCE

Some teens get involved in other types of group violence that is separate from gangs. Feelings of alienation, boredom, or rage can cause groups to form spontaneously and do violent acts. This type of violence has recently been called **wilding**.

The term was first used to identify seven teenage boys who were arrested for assaulting and raping a young woman in New York in 1989. It is now used to describe the behavior of groups of teens who wander around with nothing to do and end up doing horrible things just for the fun of it.

That has to be scary for all of us. Many of us have had the experience of getting together with friends and doing something silly or stupid just for the fun of it. But we've always managed to draw a line and stay on the right side of it.

The fact that more and more kids are stepping over the line hurts us as much as it does their victims. It increases the sense of lawlessness that is contributing to increased violence, pulling our entire society down to new lows.

Wolfpack is a term used to describe a group that forms to stalk potential robbery victims. Wilding groups tend to form randomly, but wolfpacks are organized and have a planned objective. Unlike the gangs that form organizations and demand specific loyalties from members, however, a wolfpack may form just to pull off a given robbery. Afterward, members usually disperse and may not come together again.

Riding the train is a form of violence that is most common at colleges. It involves getting a girl drunk and taking turns raping her. Since little or no physical force is involved, many of the guys who participate don't consider it rape. It's just part of the fun. But that is a rationalization. The act is rape, which is an act of violence, not sex.

FAMILY VIOLENCE

Before closing a discussion of types of violence, we need to look at family violence. Former Director of the Federal Bureau of Investigation J. Edgar Hoover once suggested that the cure for violent crime lies "not in the electric chair but in the high chair."

When you consider the long-range effects of family violence and child abuse, you begin to understand what Hoover meant.

A study of inmates at the federal penitentiary at San Quentin, California, who had been convicted of violent crimes found that one hundred percent of them had experienced some form of extreme family violence between the ages of one and ten.

Studies of murderers and assassins show that they experienced more frequent and severe child abuse than did their fellows who did not turn to violent crime.

Family violence is not self-contained, but unfortunately tends to repeat itself. Children who are abused often grow up to be abusers. Sons of abusing husbands usually grow up to become husbands who abuse their wives. Violent criminals come out of a history of violence.

Child abuse, one of the most serious forms of family violence, has not always been classified as criminal. One reason it was excluded was respect for privacy; what went on in people's homes was considered their business, not the business of government or law-enforcement officials.

Another reason child abuse was ignored for so long was a wide belief in harsh physical discipline. Most American parents through the 1950s still supported the maxim, "Spare the rod and spoil the child." It was believed that physical discipline was the only way to tame unruly children. If some of the discipline got out of hand, that was unfortunate.

As the old attitude gave way to better methods of discipline, child abuse began to be recognized for what it is. When cases began to be documented and studied, the results caused great concern.

In *Behind Closed Doors*, sociologists Murry Straus, Richard Gelles, and Suzanne Steinmetz concentrate on the extent of family violence. The facts are astounding:

- In 1975 about 46 million children between the ages of three and seventeen were living at home with both parents. Between 1 and 1.9 million of those

children had been kicked, bitten, or punched by one or both parents during that year.
- In 1975 between 275,000 and 750,000 of the 46 million children had been "beaten up" by one or both parents.
- In 1975 the parents of roughly 46,000 children, or one in every 100, used or attempted to use guns or knives on them. In most cases, the child in question was a boy. Daughters, however, received a large percentage of the kicks, bites, and punches.

Once the problem of child abuse was recognized, one would think solutions could have been found and the incidence reduced. On the contrary, it has continued to be a growing problem, and it is not limited to physical abuse. Emotional and mental abuse have similar damaging effects on children.

Violence among family members stems from many factors. Part of our human tradition has always fostered male dominance. The man is the head of the household, the authority. For too long, men were allowed to physically chastise their wives and children.

Another factor is frustration stemming from financial or other stress. In *The Hitting Habit*, Jeanne Deschner presents facts supporting her findings that the most physical violence occurs in low-income families. She makes the point that ". . . poverty in itself doesn't lead to violence in a society where everyone is poor together." The potential for violence increases when poor families are more aware of what they lack. Their frustration level increases when they can readily see the comforts others are enjoying that are not available to them.

The cycle of family violence is very difficult to break. Kids learn what they are exposed to, and if they are exposed only to violence, that is what they think is normal or right. Generally by the age of eight a child develops a "world view," says psychologist Margaret Singh. "What they see happening around them is what they expect to happen and what they believe is their role."

As a very general example, Ms. Singh says, in a home where the husband abuses the wife, a daughter may grow up to be a victim and a son to be an abuser.

To break that pattern, Ms. Singh says, young people need to gain a different viewpoint. They need to discover that there are other options in life than the ones they were taught at home. This can be done through individual counseling, group therapy, or support groups.

When considering family violence, it is important to remember its social effect.

As a simple yet stark example, imagine people who get a puppy and tie it up in the backyard. Every day that puppy is kicked and hit until it grows up to be a mean dog. Then this large dog becomes a menace to them and the whole neighborhood, attacking anyone who comes near it. And they wonder why.

That is what happens to too many kids, and the parents wonder why their children end up in prison or worse.

CHAPTER 3

Make My Day

IN THE FACE OF VIOLENCE
Violence is here
In the world of the sane,
And violence is a symptom.
I hear it in the headlong weeping of men
who have failed
I see it in the terrible dreams of boys
whose adolescence repeats all history.
—Jacob Bronowski

The poem suggests that violence is as much a part of our humanity as everything else we do, and unfortunately it is true. From earliest civilization, history is full of accounts of our violent acts toward one another. Behavioral scientists have long recognized that mankind is violent in different ways from other animals, but determining exactly why has been a difficult challenge.

Many experts believe that violence is an inborn trait, that people are naturally aggressive toward each other. Others do not support that belief, however.

In *A Sign for Cain*, Frederic Wertham, M.D., writes

that human violence is very different from an instinct. He considers a natural instinct as something positive. Our natural urges—to eat, for instance—are positive things for positive results. Violence, according to Wertham, is involved with negative factors.

One of those negative factors is aggression. Simply defined, **aggression is behavior aimed at hurting another physically or emotionally**. Psychologists define aggression as violent, angry, hostile, and destructive behavior. Sometimes the aggression is turned against people. Sometimes it is directed against objects by vandals who trash schools or paint graffiti on public buildings. Aggression can also turn inward, leading to suicide.

Even though aggression is an accepted way of life among most species of animals, we cannot apply the same acceptance to people. True, we are categorized as animals, but we are also much more sophisticated and complicated. We have elements of reasoning and emotion that lift us out of a simple category and a simple explanation for our actions.

When animals hunt and kill for food, it is purely a natural response to the instinct for survival. Some of us may find that action distasteful. We may even cringe if we see it on a nature show, but we cannot deny a certain "rightness" in the overall scheme of things.

Studies have proved that animals are governed by inhibitions that keep them from killing their own kind; a built-in safety device prevents it.

In his book *On Aggression*, behavioral scientist Konrad Lorenz explains that man does not have that safety device because we do not have the natural weapons other animals do. The lion has claws, the wolf has teeth, whereas our ability to kill relies on other weapons.

The lion refrains from using its claws on another lion as

a way of safeguarding the species. If animals attacked within their own species, they would all quickly become extinct. Had man been born with natural weapons, perhaps we also would have inhibitions that would keep us from killing each other.

But that is not the only reason people kill each other. After years of studying human behavior, psychologist Erich Fromm believes that man, in contrast to animals, is the only one who can feel intense pleasure in killing and torture. He also believes that man's destructiveness is not part of "human nature," nor is it common to all men.

Aggressive violence in people is distinguished by intent. I **intend** to get my way even if it means hurting someone else. I **intend** to get satisfaction for an injustice even if it means hurting someone else. I **intend** to eliminate that person I see as my enemy.

Other animals do not go through that reasoning process. They simply hunt and kill to eat, and fight to protect themselves.

TYPES OF AGGRESSION

Let us examine the various types of aggression.

Accidental aggression is something that hurts another person but was not intended to; for example, a hunting accident when a gun misfires, or sports-related accidents.

Playful aggression occurs when a person uses a weapon or violence as an exercise in skill and someone else is hurt. Sparring during karate or tae kwan do is a good example. Both are defense-oriented martial arts, but sometimes contact is made and an injury occurs.

Self-assertive aggression is used when a person moves toward a goal without undue hesitation, doubt, or fear. In the business world, people are said to be aggressive when they accomplish more than others. They are characterized as driven, motivated, and productive.

Unless this aggression is misused, it is not destructive or harmful. In fact, it is an important ingredient in achievement and success. Psychologists have also noted that people with this type of personal confidence are less likely to react with hostility when facing a defensive situation. They are generally less likely to feel threatened than people who have not developed self-assertiveness.

As an example, think about two kids in drama class. During a critique, Mike and Jack are both given some rough criticism: Their timing was off; they didn't project; they were stiff and unnatural in their roles. Mike listens quietly. You can tell he's not thrilled about the comments, but he doesn't get angry and upset.

Jack, however, immediately becomes defensive. It was distractions that threw off his timing. His projection level was fine; people just weren't listening. When that fails to work, Jack gets mad and storms out. He feels personally threatened by the criticism, whereas Mike is able to take it for what it is.

Defensive aggression is a reaction to danger or threat. The reaction can be either to run or to stand and fight. This is the type of aggression that we share most closely with other animals. It is also the one that is considered natural or instinctive. It's part of our basic need for self-preservation.

Threats against our freedom can raise strong defense reactions. And those threats need not be in the form of confinement or physical restraint. Various forms of oppression limit freedom and can cause the same frustration and anger as a cage or ropes.

Conformist aggression is not motivated by personal

choice. It is seen when people are told to be aggressive and they consider it their duty to obey orders. The most common example is military actions. In combat, soldiers shoot and kill people they don't even know, let alone have anything personally against.

Another form of aggression is unique to man. Erich Fromm calls it **malignant aggression** and defines it as an impulse to kill and torture that brings enjoyment. Man is the only animal that can kill his own species without rational gain. Examples of that kind of aggression are the things that usually make us squirm inside—brutality, child abuse, gang killings, massacres.

Aggression can either be **emotional** or **instrumental**. Emotional aggression occurs as a response, a reaction to a threat or provocation. In those situations, anger is usually the prevailing feeling. "That so-and-so stole my CD and I'm going to get him."

Instrumental aggression does not always involve anger. It is planned aggression used to attain a goal or reward. It may still include an intent to harm, which clearly classifies it as aggression and not assertiveness, but it is not highly influenced by feelings. Instrumental aggression has a sense of organization about it, and it is very much a part of group violence, from street gangs to armies.

It is clear that aggression in itself is not always bad or destructive. If we had no aggressive skills, we would be unable to protect ourselves from danger. We also would be unable to reach higher levels of achievement. But when we act aggressively, we need to be sure of our intent: Is it to help ourselves or hurt others?

To keep it all straight in our minds, it might help to separate the terms **aggressive** and **assertive**. Some people think the term aggressive is misused anyway, even by the experts who compiled the definitions above.

You may even have mistaken assertiveness for aggression in labeling some of your schoolmates. The football player who plows through the defensive line to gain a few yards may look aggressive, but his intent is not to hurt the other guys. His intent is to move the ball.

Or how about the candidate for Student Council president who is in your face all the time with campaign posters and fliers. His intent is to gain something for himself, not to hurt the other kids running for the office.

In determining what is true aggression, **intent to cause harm** is the crucial factor.

IS IT ALL IN OUR GENES?

In the ongoing professional debate whether violent aggression is learned or instinctive, some interesting points are made on both sides of the question. Some sociologists hold that some of the primitive rage reactions that lead to violent aggression are instinctive. They consider them part of the survival mechanism: We feel threatened, we strike out.

This reaction is sometimes described as "a blinding rage." Anger and frustration build up to such a force that it literally blinds us to our reasoning powers. We do things that we would not have done had we stopped and thought.

It can be an immediate response to an immediate threat, like trying to fight off two or three guys who jump us in the school parking lot. If we thought about it, there's no way we'd tangle with them, but we're mad now and we want to get in a few licks.

A blinding rage can also build up over time until it explodes in violence. Mass murders are prime examples to consider. The men who took guns into a McDonalds (July 18, 1984, California) or Luby's Cafeteria (October 16, 1991, Texas) and randomly opened fire were reacting to years of accumulated anger.

Sociologists recognize that most of the time people are out of control when they are involved in violence. Certainly people who commit a massacre have lost all ability to reason.

But while we can explain man's aggressive violence, we have to be careful not to excuse it. Accepting it as a fact of life only allows it to continue and escalate.

Erich Fromm says that some people prefer to believe aggression is all instinctive. In that way they don't have to consider how social problems have contributed to a rise in violence.

If it were all purely instinctive, however, we would all react the same way in certain situations, and clearly we don't. That does not mean that one reaction is always right and the other always wrong; it just means we're different.

Consider, for example, two friends who are walking around the stadium at a football game. Some known gang members start hassling them, trying to get money from them. One boy is willing to give them the money and walk away. He doesn't want any part of a fight. The other boy would rather fight than back down, even though he knows he doesn't stand a chance.

Why is one boy ready to walk away while the other isn't? According to Fromm, the reason has to do with character and experience. When we respond to a situation, we are not limited to the influence of the moment. We bring to it everything we have learned.

There are two possible explanations why the first boy wouldn't fight. He might not have had much success in using aggression to achieve his goals, so he makes a quick evaluation and decides, "It didn't work before, so why try again."

Or he might have learned to control his responses to things that only made problems worse. He had some measure of control over the situation by being able to reason that fighting was not going to help. The other guys would still end up with the money, and he'd end up with a lot of pain. "It isn't worth it."

As for the other boy, perhaps his life experience had taught him that aggression can be successful. Perhaps his parents had praised his ability to use aggression to achieve his goals, and it made him feel more manly: "Only a wimp would back down from a fight."

Each of these reactions could be labeled right or wrong, depending on your personal code. You might think the guy who walked away was right because he had the good sense to recognize a hopeless situation. Or you might think it was wrong for him to let the other guys take advantage of him.

You could also think the second guy was right for sticking up for himself, for not being a wimp. On the other hand, you might consider that it was stupid of him to try to fight back against such odds.

How you judge those actions depends on your experience and attitudes. Like the boys, you will make a decision that may be right only for you.

In thinking about all this, it's easy to see how we are influenced by our own experience and attitudes. It adds considerable weight to the belief that our behavior is determined more by environment than by instincts.

For a long time one of the principal arguments for the

heredity theory was the fact that aggressive violence is primarily associated with males:

- All the documented mass murders from 1949 to 1991 in the U.S. were committed by men.
- Most of the world's greatest atrocities were planned and carried out by men.
- Over ninety percent of all violent crime is committed by men.

Does that mean that men are born with some abnormal gene that sets them apart from women? Not necessarily. Even though some behavioral scientists believed that in the early years of studying human nature, modern scientists reject it. Now it is believed that men and women start out basically the same, and it's how they are brought up that makes the difference.

In a column in the *Dallas Morning News*, Peter Riga, a former professor of law and theology, wrote, "Males are taught that it is manly to fight, to kill. To beat the other fellow, in whatever way, is to be courageous, strong, masculine. Nonviolence is sissy, cowardly, unmanly—even womanly."

That basic attitude, or variations of it, has been a dominant influence since the beginning of history.

WILL IT EVER CHANGE?

We can't control aggressive violence by law or morality. Both have been in existence for centuries, and man is still aggressive. Does that mean we are hopelessly destined to continue down a path perhaps leading to our destruction?

Perhaps not. Konrad Lorenz offers a few suggestions for ways to stem the tide.

The first is a personal challenge to each individual to **develop an awareness of himself**. "Know yourself," Lorenz says, "so you can govern yourself."

Have you ever thought about what you might do in a potentially violent situation? What if you were one of the boys threatened at the football game? What would you do? What would be right for you, and why?

Thinking through that now could help ensure that you do make the decision that is right for you. It can also help you not to make a hasty decision when you are confronted with a sudden situation.

The second suggestion Lorenz offers is to **know others**. Gaining a deeper understanding of human behavior can help us not to feel threatened by what would otherwise seem strange. Lorenz also believes that something as simple as knowing each other better will kindle friendship, not hostility.

Examples are learning about other races and cultures through groups at school, or having neighborhood block parties so people are not strangers. The more we find we have in common, the less we see others as a threat.

The final suggestion is to **find genuine causes to serve** in society. We all have a little of what Lorenz calls "militant enthusiasm" that can be used either positively or negatively. If we channel that enthusiasm into aggression, it does nothing good for society. It just pulls us apart. If we use it positively, it can pull us together.

Wanting to react with aggression to certain situations is a perfectly normal human response. Whether out of instinct or from learned behavior, it is still something most of us do. A guy shoves us in the hallway and we get mad. We want to shove him back. Wanting to shove him isn't wrong, but acting on that impulse is.

So what do we do? Do we let all that anger build up until it explodes? Do we let people push us around and just take it?

We consider those questions in detail in Chapter 10 but two things are worth looking at now.

The first is the importance of redirecting your aggression. You get mad at the guy who shoved you, but instead of shoving him back, you hit some inanimate object. Sometimes you can blow off steam by going for a long run, or kicking a soccer ball around. It's even okay to think of the soccer ball as the person who made you mad.

Another factor in controlling aggression comes from elements of sports. Lorenz considers most sports to be controlled aggression, and one can see his point.

Football is an extremely aggressive sport. If there were no rules or control, no telling how violent it might become. But even in impromptu games, a certain level of sportsmanship and fair play keeps players from hurting each other seriously.

That is not to deny the existence of dirty players, and some dirty coaches who encourage players to "take out" an opponent. But they are the exception. Most players adhere to a code of conduct.

If you have participated in organized sports, you probably have that sense of sportsmanship and fair play. There may even have been times when that sense has kept you from smearing some guy across the soccer field.

Lorenz ties that sense into his suggestion to "know yourself." He sees sports as a way for people to learn how to be aware of and control their own fighting behavior. He also sees major sporting events such as the Olympics as a way to diminish aggression on a larger scale. "The Olympic Games are virtually the only occasion when the anthem of one nation can be played without arousing any hostility against another," he writes.

The reason it works is because each team is as dedicated to the ideals of sportsmanship as to their national enthusiasm.

Maybe that's one of the reasons the Olympic Games are so popular. It makes us feel good to see friendly competition between countries that are traditionally considered enemies. We recognize the ideals that make this possible, and it gives us the feeling that all is not hopeless.

Kids and Guns

I n a single week, the following headlines appeared in a major metropolitan newspaper:

GIRL, 15, WOUNDED IN CLASH OF RIVAL GROUPS OUTSIDE SCHOOL

15-YEAR-OLD INDICTED IN SLAYING

2 TEENAGERS INDICTED IN KILLINGS OF 4 AT RESTAURANT

And those were only the incidents that made the papers. How many other teens have guns and use them routinely to threaten and intimidate others?

The fact that kids with guns are an escalating problem cannot be ignored. Headlines in newspapers across the nation shout it every day, and concern about the availability of guns grows.

A segment of the prime-time TV show "Street Stories" (January 23, 1992) presented the problem from a variety of angles. It opened with students arriving at a Florida school for a routine that is becoming all too familiar at high schools in every state. Security officers took the students into the gym, where they had to put everything they were carrying on tables. Their belongings were then searched while the students lined up for individual screening with metal detectors.

One girl was arrested for having a .38 revolver in her purse.

Then the scene shifted to the streets, where kids were interviewed at random. Some showed off scars from bullet wounds from past confrontations, but the scars didn't make them consider giving up the guns. "Ya gotta have it, man. It's protection."

Guns are available for as little as $15, and they're not hard to get. Tom Jones, a youth counselor, said that kids as young as nine have guns, and any kind of gun is available as long as the money is there. A seventeen-year-old was shown buying a machine gun while other kids as young as six or seven watched. His reason for buying such a weapon? "Everyone says you gotta have one to be safe."

That is why fourteen-year-old Vince W. had a gun: To protect himself. He never had any intention of using it.

Vince grew up in a wealthy part of town. In the summer of 1990, he and his friends got in a fight with some other kids. One kid punched Vince in the nose, and Vince grabbed his gun and fired six shots. He killed one boy and wounded another. Now Vince lives in prison. He went straight from eighth grade to a twelve-year sentence.

Vince looks more like "Mr. Prep School" than a "streetwise punk," which points up the fact that the problem of kids and guns has no boundaries of color, class, or economics. "It could happen to anybody," Vince said. "Anybody who's having problems with kids at school. Get scared. Turn the way I did."

Asked if he understood what it meant to kill, whether he had ever thought about it before, he said no. "I didn't even think about it. I didn't think I was ever going to kill anybody. I didn't want to take that kid's life. It didn't seem fair to me that I did. It was all like a movie thing to see someone die. But I didn't think it could ever happen to me."

Guns have always been associated with power, especially masculine power. Only a little over a century ago, guns were a necessity for reasons much different from today's reasons. People hunted with guns to provide food for their families. Guns were used for protection against threats from the wilderness. People who could handle guns well were often the most respected men in town. Through their ability, they had power and control.

It is that same drive for power and control that motivates so many young people today to carry a gun. "It's their security blanket," according to Cookie Rodriguez, founder of Street Church Academy in Dallas.

Ms. Rodriguez, who was quoted in an article by Nancy Kruh in the *Dallas Morning News* (September 23, 1991), added that many teens think having a gun will make others afraid of them, give them the upper hand.

That need for strength and power was the predominant motive for having a gun, according to the teens Ms. Kruh interviewed. But, like Vince, those teens often failed to realize the full scope of using a gun. One fourteen-year-old boy admitted having been involved in a number of drive-by shootings. He told the reporter that "he quit when it dawned on him that he actually might kill someone."

Another boy told Ms. Kruh that he has barely known most of the people he has shot. "I guess if I really got to know them," he said, "I wouldn't be shooting them."

Most states have laws forbidding the sale of guns to anyone under eighteen. The laws also forbid anyone of any age to carry a concealed weapon without a permit. But neither the laws nor law enforcement are able to keep kids and guns apart.

Kids carry all types of guns, from cheap pistols to Uzis or 9mm automatics. Weapons that take clips are preferred because they hold more bullets and can be reloaded faster than revolvers.

The most common reason kids carry guns is for protection. "The street institution says if somebody hits you or shoots you, nine times out of ten you won't see the police there," says Zachary Thompson, director of a community center. "So you have to protect yourself." The fallacy of that reasoning is that it merely compounds the problem. The more the violence grows, the more kids feel that they have to have a gun, even kids who never thought about it before.

Another reason kids carry guns is as a status symbol. In some neighborhoods, having a gun is as prestigious as wearing the latest sports shoes.

For some young people, a gun is simply a quick means to an end: the easiest and most convenient way to solve a problem.

Whatever the reason, more and more kids are carrying weapons. In Dallas alone, the police department's school liaison unit confiscates an average of three guns a day. Youth Division Detective Sam Schiller considers the situation tragic. "Kids just don't understand that guns are dangerous."

In a 1991 study of five high schools in Seattle, 34

percent of the students reported having easy access to guns. Many students said they owned guns, and most said they had taken them to school. Of those owners, 33 percent said they had shot at another person at some time. The study concluded that there is an association between gun ownership and the high rates of homicide, suicide, and unintentional deaths.

Other national surveys have reported that one in five high school students had carried a gun, knife, or club to school or elsewhere. In response to this growing problem, Robert Rubel, director of the National Alliance for Safe Schools, Bethesda, Maryland, had this to say, "Fifty, twenty, even ten years ago, kids in school settled differences by fighting. Nowadays, especially in our larger cities, they don't fight. They shoot."

One reason so many teens are shooting is that guns are so easy to come by. As Tim related in Chapter 1, if you want a gun you can get it if you know whom to ask or where to look. Guns acquired in burglaries are always for sale, and young people on dope frequently steal them to make money to support their habit. Drug dealers are also a source of guns, often giving a gun as payment for making a run.

Despite the laws prohibiting the sale of weapons to minors, some pawnshops are willing to risk the consequences for a profit, and word spreads quickly about those shops.

Some teens steal guns from their own homes. They may even stage a burglary to make it look as if someone had broken into the house. Those guns can then be offered for sale, trade, or loan.

No one can deny that the widespread availability of guns is a serious problem. Some people think a solution is to have metal detectors in every school. But one teen said the detectors "are demeaning. It's like walking into a prison."

More metal detectors might minimize the gun problem in the schools, but it wouldn't do anything about the availability on the streets. If a gun is confiscated at school, a person can just buy another one.

This easy access to guns was the subject of an article by Jim Dwyer in New York *Newsday* (March 2, 1992). Dwyer based his story on the manufacture and distribution of cheap handguns by a California company, Raven Arms, owned by George Jennings. "Raven Arms wholesales the MP-25 for $29.75," Dwyer wrote. "Gun retailers pay less than $35.00 for it. They then sell it for under $70.00, and from there it gets into the hands of the children who are blowing apart their own generation and anyone who gets in the way."

Dwyer's main point was that this company and the people who are getting rich at the expense of all these lives ought to be held accountable. "The Jenningses spend $13 [to manufacture the Raven 25-caliber semiautomatic], make $15 or $16 in profit, and the rest of us pick up the pieces, a million dollars at a time."

Dwyer separates the issue of gun control from accountability. There is a need for both, but accountability strikes closer to the heart of things. In New York, State Assembly members Dan Feldman and Roger Green have introduced a bill that would hold manufacturers of assault weapons liable for their products. If someone were killed by a Raven, the company would have to pay damages. On the surface, this might seem to be merely shifting the blame. After all, aren't the people who pull the trigger ultimately responsible? Yes, they are. But before they pull a trigger, they have to get one. If guns were not so accessible, fewer triggers would be pulled.

It is estimated that 200 million firearms are distributed among the civilian population of the United States. Handguns now outsell rifles and shotguns, and the gun of choice is the semiautomatic with a magazine holding ten to fifteen cartridges. Some of these weapons are in the hands of responsible hunters and people who shoot for sport, but many of them are not. Many of them are in the hands of criminals who shoot indiscriminately and children who don't think before they pull the trigger.

DO WE OR DON'T WE?

The issue of gun control is highly controversial. The Constitution gives us the "right . . . to keep and bear arms," and some people will go to their grave to defend that right. But what we have lost between the Constitution and modern times is respect and responsibility.

In those times when guns were a part of life and survival, there was awareness of the purpose and power of a gun. It could kill, so you had better be sure you knew what you were aiming at. As young people were introduced to weapons, they were taught about proper use and safety. Most important, they were taught to respect the power of a gun. They knew that guns killed.

Some people who oppose gun control argue that "guns don't kill, people do." That is true. But if people didn't have such instant access to guns, wouldn't it make a difference?

MAYBE IT WOULD

In Canada, the teen violence rate is much lower than in the U.S., and the gun laws are much stricter. To own a rifle or long-barreled gun in Canada, a person must first obtain a Firearms Acquisition Certificate. The minimum age to apply is eighteen, and applicants are put through a rigorous screening process.

Part of the screening is to determine whether the applicant has a history of violence. Two references must be supplied. Friends, neighbors, and relatives are interviewed, and if the applicant has ever threatened anyone, the application is denied.

Other requirements of the law include passing a gun safety and education program, and a twenty-eight-day delay between approval and issuance of the certificate.

For handguns or short-barrel weapons, the rules are even stricter. There is a special registry for this type of firearm, and applicants have to state a specific purpose for ownership. Acceptable purposes include being a gun collector or a member of an authorized target-shooting club. Owners also have to abide by safe storage and transport guidelines.

The Canadian gun laws also have severe controls on firepower. They prohibit fully automatic and converted automatics and limit the size of magazines.

Most of these restrictions took effect in 1978, and according to James Hayes, Coordinator of the Firearms Control Task Group at the Department of Justice, they have reduced violent crime considerably. Homicides went down, suicides declined, and armed robbery dropped significantly.

"Gun control is always a divisive issue," Hayes said, "But there's no question guns are dangerous to public safety. The Minister and Parliament were quite courageous in pushing for these controls. And recent surveys show that 60 to 80 percent of the people support strong gun control. Forty percent even support banning guns completely."

One advantage Canada has over the United States is that their system of government is not so strongly influenced by lobbyists. The Shooting Federation of Canada, which is similar to our National Rifle Association (NRA), did not have the power to prevent the gun control laws in 1978.

One of the major arguments against gun control in the U.S. is that it won't work: People who want guns will still get them. It won't reduce crime and violence; it will only prevent law-abiding citizens from having weapons.

Before we agree with that argument, let's consider some figures from the Canadian Centre for Justice Statistics suggesting that perhaps it would work.

In 1990 there were 656 homicides, of which 49 were committed by juveniles between the ages of twelve and seventeen. Of the 269,440 crimes of violence reported, 15,705 were committed by juveniles.

Those statistics are significantly lower than figures for the U.S. According to the Coalition to Stop Gun Violence, handguns were used in 11,750 murders in the United States in 1990. The number of suicides stood at 12,000, and 639,000 violent crimes were committed. Even more startling is the fact that gunshot wounds to children of sixteen and under have increased by 300 percent since 1986.

Columnist Bob Greene wrote in the *Chicago Tribune*, (March 1, 1992), "This country is in the process of shooting itself to death." He went on to cite the statistics given above.

Greene's concern is shared by a growing number of people, and for some it leads to drastic measures. One woman who wrote to Ann Landers (January 1992) had moved her family several times in the United States to get away from schools where her kids were harassed. "They were beaten up and robbed so many times they were afraid to leave the house." Out of desperation when she discovered her son was carrying a knife to defend himself, she took the family to Canada. "No school anywhere is perfect these days," she said. "But in Canada, I do not fear for the lives of my children every time they walk out of the house."

GUN CONTROL IN THE U.S.?

Whether or not we will ever have gun control in the United States is a wide-open issue and a very volatile one. Many gun owners, especially members of the NRA, are adamant in their opposition to controls. Joining forces with them are the gun manufacturers. "To blame the gun for its misuse is to avoid dealing with the real issue," says Ronald E. Stillwell of the Colt Manufacturing Company in Connecticut. "The issue is poverty, drugs, and jobs."

Other opinions include the thought that seeking gun control is just a way to excuse the failure of the court system to deal harshly with criminals.

On the other side of the argument is the chilling reality that the problem is getting out of control by sheer volume alone. Jeffrey Y. Muchnik, legislative director of the Coalition to Stop Gun Violence, urges a reduction in the manufacture of guns. "The more guns we have," he says, "the more people get shot and killed."

Guns and gun-related violence are also a major concern for C. Everett Koop, former Surgeon General of the U.S. Public Health Service. Writing in the *Journal of the American Medical Association* (June 10, 1992), he and George D. Lundberg, MD, urged gun control and responsibility, calling violence the fastest-growing public health problem in the country.

To combat the problem, they challenged the Public Health Service to take an active role in seeking solutions. They asked for major research on the causes, prevention, and cures of violence and for legislation to reverse the upward trend of firearm injuries and deaths.

Comparing the right to own a gun with the right to own and operate a motor vehicle, Drs. Koop and Lundberg wrote that both rights carry with them responsibilities. To insure responsibility in firearm ownership, all owners should meet specific criteria:

- Be of a certain age and physical/mental condition.
- Demonstrate knowledge and skill in use of that firearm.
- Be monitored in the firearm's use.
- Forfeit the right to own or operate the firearm if the conditions are negated.

Support of gun control is not a popular position, and it has been a difficult battle for some. James Brady, former White House press secretary, was wounded in the 1981 attempted assassination of President Ronald Reagan. Along with his wife, Sarah, Brady has devoted the last ten years to promoting proposed legislation called the Brady Handgun Violence Prevention Act.

Known by the more familiar name "Brady Bill," the act would require a seven-day waiting period for purchase of a gun. During that time, gun dealers could provide law-enforcement officials with information about the person for a background check.

In 1988 the Brady Bill was defeated in the House of Representatives; it did not gain approval until three years later, and it still has to pass the Senate before it can be sent to the President for signature.

The whole issue of gun control revolves around rights. Sports enthusiasts don't want to lose their right to have guns for hunting or target shooting "Why should I relinquish my right to have a target pistol because of the irresponsibility of others?" says an NRA member, Robert J. "That's not a satisfactory solution to the problem."

While Robert is against severe restrictions, he is in favor of licensing and some other controls. "People should have some sort of safety training," he says. "They should know how to use guns and how to store them. Guns should be kept in locked cases. That would discourage kids from getting hold of Dad's gun."

Robert agrees that banning guns and enforcing the ban would help to solve the immediate problems of violence. In simple mathematical terms, the fewer the guns, the fewer the violent crimes. But he thinks some of the other problems should be attacked. "Let's do something about drugs," he says. "Maybe so many kids wouldn't be shooting each other if they weren't strung out on dope."

Robert also thinks more has to be done to teach young people responsibility and the consequences of what they do. "Kids need to be taught that for every action there is a reaction. For me it was a choice. If I do this, that will be the punishment. Do I want to take the risk? It is worth it? Do I want to accept the consequences?"

At age twenty-three, Robert is not so far removed from his teenage years that he can't remember how much he hated his parents' strictness and how he fought against it. But now he is grateful. "It was definitely good for me. Sort of like eating the right food. The positive effects don't show up until later."

*　　　*　　　*

Kris, a sixteen-year-old high school student, doesn't think gun control is a solution to the violence problem. "It's like Prohibition," he says. "If someone wants to get a gun, he can."

But Kris does agree that some kinds of controls would help. "We need to be stricter about who guns are sold to. People with a history of violent mental problems should be prohibited."

Katie, a seventeen-year-old high school senior also wants a waiting period for buying a gun. "That way there'd be better control over who has guns. During the waiting period, background checks could be done. Then the people who are dangerous wouldn't be able to get a gun so easily."

Perhaps the strongest argument for gun control comes from the realization that so many innocent people suffer. In the next chapter we shall look at victims of violence.

CHAPTER 5

Who Pays the Price?

"One of the bargains men make with one another in order
to maintain their sanity is to share an illusion that they are
safe even when the physical evidence in the world around
them does not seem to warrant that conclusion."
—Kai T. Erikson, *Everything in Its Path*

Fear is becoming as much a part of the American
culture as football, pizza, and slumber parties.
People are afraid to go out at night, even in their
own neighborhoods, and even school isn't a place you can
feel safe anymore.

Why?

Because of violence.

There is something very frightening about the possibility of violence at the hands of a stranger, but that
possibility is more and more a part of some people's
reality.

It would be nice if we could somehow isolate violence.
If people wanted to fight each other, they could do so
without involving us or other innocent bystanders. But
the truth is that hundreds of people are killed or injured
just for being in the wrong place at the wrong time.

That happened late one night to eighteen-year-old Ronald, who was driving home. He was shot by an unknown gunman who may have been trying to steal his car.

In a newspaper interview, Ronald's mother said they had talked frequently about the dangers on the street, but Ronald never thought anything could happen to him because he never did anything to get in trouble. He just went out that night for a little fun. What he got was a bullet in his back that left him paralyzed from the waist down.

There are hundreds of stories like Ronald's in hundreds of cities across the nation—stories about teens who went out cruising and ended up with more than they bargained for.

As unfortunate as those incidents are, the young victims tell the most poignant stories. Children and even babies have been in the way of stray bullets from gang fights or random violence. In some neighborhoods mothers fear for the safety of their children every time they hear a loud noise.

A television special titled "Prime Time Oprah" (March, 1991) dealt with the effects of violence on some people. The participants were nine-year-old children who had been victims of or witnesses to violence in their neighborhood, school, or home.

All the children expressed fear, anxiety, and terrible sadness. Some talked about how the anger begins to build in them and they want to strike back. The unfortunate fact is that many of them *will* begin to strike back.

Most young people involved with violence have themselves been victims. Part of the motivation for their violent acts is wanting to get back at someone, or to show someone they can't be taken advantage of.

Sometimes violence is a horrible family legacy. As we

saw in Chapter 2, children who have been abused grow up to be abusers and often turn to violent crime.

THE RIPPLE EFFECT

One can be a victim of violent crime, or a drive-by shooting, or simply a tragic accident. With more and more handguns in homes, incidents of accidental shooting are growing, and they are not limited to the largest cities in the United States.

A story in the Birmingham (Alabama) *News* (April 8, 1991) told of a twelve-year-old boy who accidentally shot his fifteen-year-old brother. The boy found a gun in a drawer in his home and started playing with it. His brother tried to take the gun away, and it went off. Three hours later he died.

Children's Hospital in Birmingham treated seven child victims of accidental shootings from January through April 1991. In all of 1990 they had treated a total of fourteen, and one nurse is very concerned about the increase. "It's a growing problem," she said. "Other pediatric units in big cities like Washington, D.C., have seen the increase long before we have. People never think it will happen to them. But if they were to see what the kids in our trauma center have to go through, they wouldn't think twice about getting rid of the gun or locking it up."

The tragedy of homicide, suicide, and accidental shooting goes far beyond the moment. Each victim had family and friends who shared in the pain of the incidents, for some a pain that will never go away.

Some families of murder victims have tried to find constructive and helpful ways to ease their pain.

In May 1991, relatives of three murder victims talked to a group of teenage boys at Dallas House, a halfway house for youths who have been in trouble. Each relative spoke in deliberate, heart-wrenching detail about the pain, the sense of loss.

"Now when I need a hug, I don't have anybody to hug," Pat Matthews said. "I have a picture of [her daughter] in my bedroom. And when I look at that picture and say 'I love you,' she can't say I love you back."

Ms. Matthews' sixteen-year-old daughter, Nikki, was murdered on July 18, 1989. Ms. Matthews first reaction was disbelief and denial, which quickly turned to anger. She told reporter Frank Trejo of the Dallas *Morning News* that she was so angry at God that she couldn't sit through church services without bursting into tears and running out.

To make sure the boys understood the permanence of her loss, she concluded: "Now for the rest of my life, for the rest of my mama's life, for the rest of my family's life, we will never have Nikki back with us."

What effect this victims' awareness program will have on the overall problem of violence is still unknown. But treatment coordinator Robert Louis, who started the program at Dallas House, is optimistic. "I think this really has the potential to do a lot of good," he said.

Patsy Day, founder of Victims Outreach, and one of the three-member panel to talk to the boys, believes that with the right approach some kids can be turned away from a life of violence.

"We know there are people who are capable of being rehabilitated," she said. "With juveniles in particular, sometimes their offenses are the beginning of a life of crime because they are not thinking of the consequences. They've seen so much sanitized violence on television, where there is no blood and no one really dies. What we try to do is educate them as to what kind of pain they can cause through one thoughtless moment or one intentionally mean moment."

Ms. Day also made the point that she has worked very hard not to let the experience of losing her daughter turn her into a hate-filled person. "If I do that, I'm allowing the person who killed her to control the rest of my life," she said. "If I become what he is, then he's won the battle."

That was an important message for the boys gathered that night. Many of them were in the halfway house because of reactions to some situation over which they had no control. They needed to hear that you can take control. You can make choices that are positive instead of negative, even if you, too, have been a victim.

More Innocent Victims

A feature story, "Children in the Crossfire," by Nancy Kruh, told of twenty-six episodes of senseless violence during the month of July 1991 that left four children dead and twenty-two wounded (Dallas *Morning News*, September 22, 1991).

The victims included a five-year-old girl who was mistakenly shot by a drug dealer, a two-year-old hit by a bullet that came ripping through her apartment wall, and a swimming pool full of children whom a fourteen-year-old boy used for target practice.

Why devote over four full pages of newsprint to such sad, senseless stories? Because they are just that— senseless, leaving another group of relatives and friends trying to cope.

The mother of a fourteen-year-old boy who was accidentally shot by a friend only wanted to know why. Why did they *have* the gun? Why didn't the friend know it was loaded? The friend had no satisfactory answers. He had the gun because he thought it made him "cool." He thought they had already used up all the bullets shooting at stop signs. He wouldn't have turned it on his friend if he had known a bullet was still in the chamber. But he didn't think. He didn't check. And now his friend is dead. In a way, he is a victim as well. He has to live with the memory of killing his friend.

IN THE LONGER RANGE

In addition to the obvious consequences of violence, some effects are harder to measure and are more damaging to society as a whole.

It is easy to see that we all pay some kind of price for the violence around us. We pay the salaries of law-enforcement personnel. We foot the bill for new prisons. We pay court costs, legal fees for prosecution, and very often for defense through the public defender's office.

What is not so easy to see is the price we pay as members of a society that is slowly breaking down.

Professor Keith Haley, Coordinator of the Criminal Justice Department at Collin County (Texas) Community College, believes that as violence increases we are no longer bound together by mutual trust and respect. He explains that a person who is a victim of violent crime naturally is more fearful, especially of strangers. "The victim passes that fear on to family and friends. And perpetuating that fear makes us all more tentative."

That fear and uncertainty makes us pull inward, separating us in degrees from people with whom we would otherwise interact. That can create mistrust and the potential for more crime and violence.

To understand fully Professor Haley's point, let's put it

in terms of family relationship. Suppose you live in a family with an abusive mother. In moments of uncontrolled frustration and anger, she beats you and you never understand why. Because of her abuse, you become more afraid and unsure of yourself and her. Sometimes you wish you could talk to her, but you're afraid. What if it just makes her mad again? So you don't do it. You grow up in a terrible situation that is never resolved because you've turned inward. The mistrust and misunderstanding are still there, and the violence will probably continue.

The family has always been considered the backbone of society because the way we function in that little group largely determines the way we operate in larger groups. How we treat each other and how we approach problems are very similar.

In the case of community violence or school violence, the same pattern emerges. If someone threatens you at school, fear takes over, and the fear brings uncertainty. There's no way you can talk to that person. There's no way you can even find out what the problem is, let alone solve it. So it remains to spawn more problems.

Sociologist Kai T. Erikson says that a victim develops "a sense of vulnerability, a feeling that one has lost a certain natural immunity to misfortune, a growing conviction, even, that the world is no longer a safe place to be."

Victims feel that way long after the incident of violence has passed. They end up living with a fear that affects everything they do in life.

To help break this cycle of victimization, fear, and uncertainty, Professor Haley's department has increased its efforts to address the needs of victims. This includes support groups, counseling, better communications during investigations, and greater respect during the whole process.

"Victims need to know someone cares about them," Professor Haley says, "and cares about what happened to them. This understanding can help them deal with the anger and the fear so they're not trapped by it."

The main thing that sets victims of criminal violence apart from the rest of us is not that something bad happened to them. Bad things of varying degrees happen to all of us, but eventually we recover and get on with our lives. But victims have absolutely no control over what happened to them. That, in turn, makes them feel even more out of control.

We can take certain precautions against other misfortunes in life. We can drive carefully to avoid accidents. We can make sure a ladder is sturdy before we step on it. We can eat right and exercise to stay healthy. But we can't do anything about the sudden unprovoked attack that comes from nowhere.

That is what happened to Joanne Roosevelt on March 2, 1990.

Four years earlier, the fifty-two-year-old woman had signed up as a sponsor in the I Have a Dream Foundation, which pairs adults with disadvantaged youths to encourage them to stay in school and out of trouble. Mrs. Roosevelt was paired with Willie Adams, and at first it worked out fine. Willie came to her house with friends, and they played pool or basketball, or enjoyed her swimming pool. Mrs. Roosevelt felt it was doing the kids some good, and she enjoyed having them. She even had pictures of herself with the kids, taken at Christmas 1989.

Willie drifted off, however, and she didn't see him again until March 2. He came to her door that day just as she was returning from work, and he had another boy with him. He said they had come by because they had missed the school bus.

Mrs. Roosevelt invited the boys in. They had some snacks and played a little pool. Then she offered to drive them home.

In a newspaper interview, Mrs. Roosevelt said that she "sensed the boys were up to something" as she drove following Willie's directions. "I just had a funny feeling," she said. "But I never once thought I'd be hurt. I trusted him."

When Mrs. Roosevelt stopped the car to let the boys out, Willie suddenly lunged at her with a knife. He stabbed her repeatedly as she struggled to get free of her seat belt and out of the car. He continued to stab her even after she had fallen to the pavement. Luckily, several people saw what was happening, and Willie ran away before he killed Mrs. Roosevelt. Even so, she suffered multiple wounds, including a punctured lung.

Her physical recovery took several months, but her emotional recovery is still going on. A year after the attack, Mrs. Roosevelt was interviewed again and said she was trying not to be bitter. She had thought about participating in the Foundation again, but she was still not sure.

That uncertainty is part of the vulnerability associated with victimization. To overcome it, psychologists recommend confronting the source of the fear. For some victims, that means going to the trial of the person who assaulted them. For others, it means returning to the scene.

On March 12, 1992, survivors of the 1991 massacre at a Luby's Cafeteria in Killeen, Texas, returned for the reopening of the restaurant. It was part of a healing process, and one woman said it was important "to see that things are normal again."

Life was anything but normal that October day when a man drove his truck through the front window of the cafeteria and killed twenty-two people, wounded twenty-three others, and then killed himself. Because of the horrifying nature of the incident, recovery has been slow for most of the survivors.

At the time of the massacre, an interview was held with Dr. Robert Pynoos, director of the program in trauma, violence, and sudden bereavement at the University of California at Los Angeles. Dr Pynoos said, "The emotional impact of a mass shooting lasts long after physical wounds heal." He encouraged other mental health professionals to be thoughtful in planning how best to deal with the emotional aftershocks of random violence. "The system needs to set up an appropriate mental health outreach and intervention." he said.

Dr. Pynoos counseled survivors of the 1984 McDonald's massacre in southern California. After that incident, the restaurant was torn down, and Dr. Pynoos didn't think it was necessarily the best thing to do. "It eliminated a reminder of the tragedy," he said, "but some survivors missed the opportunity to return to the scene. Walking through the restaurant with loved ones could have improved victims' ability to communicate what they went through."

HOW NOT TO BE A VICTIM

It may be easier to avoid being a victim than to cope with the trauma of being one. The problem is that most people do not think about it before something happens. Most of us just go about our business without being prepared for the possibility of becoming a victim.

On a television show titled "Street Smarts: How to

Avoid Being a Victim." Detective J.J. Bittenbinder talked about how important it is to have a plan. A homicide detective in Chicago, Bittenbinder told the audience that many of the crimes he investigates could have been avoided if the victim had had a plan. He also stressed that it can happen to anybody. "Don't kid yourself that it only happens to the other guy," he said. "It can happen to you. Think about what you'd do now. Don't wait until it's happening."

The program was geared toward adults and covered such crimes as burglary, robbery, and rape, but the points Bittenbinder made could be applied to the kind of violence you might encounter at school and in your neighborhood.

Bittenbinder outlined four main factors of a good plan. First, **make yourself a tougher target.** "Tough targets don't get selected. If you don't want to be prey, look like a predator. Predators are always looking up and around. Prey looks at the ground."

He recommended assuming an air and attitude of confidence. At school, that might mean walking to class with your head held high, suggesting that you are strong and in control, not weak and vulnerable.

Second, **deny privacy.** Quite simply, that means keeping the predator at a distance. Don't give him the place to do you harm. Bittenbinder encouraged people to trust their instincts in certain situations. "When you think something is wrong, it probably is," he said.

Mrs. Roosevelt might have prevented her tragedy had she followed her instincts, her "funny feeling." Even though she was driving, she let Willie control the situation. Bittenbinder explained that in the first few moments of a crime, no one has control. If you can somehow take control first, chances are you can avoid the crime entirely.

You can also avoid potentially dangerous situations at school or on the streets by not being alone. Stay with a group of friends. If you are alone and you run into a bunch of toughs, turn and walk away. "Running away is always your first, best option," Bittenbinder said.

Be aware of places that are safe and places that are not. Avoid places that are not safe like alleys and dark streets.

The third step is to **attract attention**. Yelling is good. Bittenbinder suggested not simply calling for help, but yelling "Fire!" People react differently to a call for help than when they hear "Fire!" If you call for help, they may not want to get involved. Hearing someone yelling "Fire" already involves them in a potential danger, and they are more willing to do something.

The final part of the plan is to **take action**. If you live in a tough neighborhood or go to a tough school, learn how to defend yourself. Don't be a helpless victim. Take classes in self-defense or martial arts.

If you do find yourself suddenly confronted by someone who means to do you harm and he grabs your arm, pull on his thumb. That will usually break the grip and allow you to get away. If he grabs your coat or jacket, let it be pulled off, and **run away**.

Bittenbinder stressed that running away is always the best thing to do, even if the person has a gun. A person who confronts you with a gun has probably already decided to use it. The more time you give the person, the greater the possibility. If you break and run, however, you in-crease the odds in your favor. Quoting statistics from case files, Bittenbinder said that 2 percent of the people who break and run are shot and hit; the other 98 percent are not.

NO MAN IS AN ISLAND

As important as it is to take steps to protect ourselves, we cannot isolate ourselves in safe little shells. The problem of violence will never be solved merely by learning how to protect ourselves. We have to examine ways to attack the problem on the broader scale of schools, neighborhoods, cities, and countries.

Charles Silberman, in *Criminal Violence, Criminal Justice*, writes about a "commitment to change" as one step out of the darkness. He cites the example of a delinquency prevention project in Puerto Rico that changed an entire community and reduced juvenile crime. Although the project was begun primarily to serve juveniles, it developed programs for adults as well. Silberman writes, "These programs are reshaping the tone and fabric of the entire community; in the process, the delinquency rate has been cut in half, despite an exploding teenage population."

What made this project so successful was that it went into an area mired in hopelessness, poverty, and disorganization and brought solutions such as job training and a sense of hope. Those solutions enhanced the dignity and self-respect of the people who were given the means to take control of their own lives. The more control they had, the more they cared about themselves and each other. What started as a simple project ended up changing a whole community.

Professor Haley also refers to the need for people to take action against the causes of violence. The good news is that he believes the time is not too far off when that will happen.

Perhaps it is already happening to some degree. That's why people like Pat Matthews and Patsy Day talk to troubled kids. That's why someone like Mrs. Roosevelt will consider working for disadvantaged kids again.

Just as we can get caught up in a tide of violence, we can get caught up in a tide of efforts to do something about it. We can all make a decision to be part of the solution, not part of the problem.

CHAPTER 6

Violence in the Media

"**W**e not only tolerate violence," says the renowned psychologist Karl Menninger. "We put it on the front pages of our newspapers. One third or one fourth of our television programs use it for the amusement of our children. Condone? My dear friends, we love it."

Some people would like to believe that Menninger is overreacting: There's nothing wrong with the level of violence in the media today. After all, we're dealing with a sophisticated audience that can tell reality from unreality, right from wrong.

That is the response a lot of professionals use to argue for freedom of expression in art and media. But too many people overlook how we learn to define right and wrong.

Our values, the principles by which we conduct our lives, are determined by all the things that influence us as we are growing up. To say that we are not influenced by what we see is simply not true.

For example, let's consider part of Tim's story from Chapter 1. Tim's family was primarily nonviolent. His parents did not approve of violent aggression and tried to teach the children other values. His brothers and sisters for the most part were not involved. So how did Tim learn violence? By what he saw, on the streets and on TV.

Tim says the programs he liked most were the ones like "Hunter," in which the hero always has a gun to give him the edge. "They were the ultimate," he says. "They had the power."

The question of whether the fiction made the reality seem any less real is harder for Tim to answer. "It was more like . . . like the movies, 'Make my day,' but it was happening." But after giving it more thought, Tim adds that what he saw on TV made his violent behavior seem acceptable, okay, the way to handle things.

If Tim was influenced by what he saw on TV and in the movies, how many others are as well? Is his an isolated incident? Could there be a connection between a rise in violence in the media and the rise in violence in real life? Is it time to do something about that?

Dr. Arlette Lefebvre, a child psychiatrist in Toronto, Canada, thinks it is way past time. As a member of the Children's Broadcast Institute, a national organization promoting better-quality TV, she is actively crusading against Ninja Turtle violence.

"Cartoon figures have always been violent," she said in a newspaper article (May 26, 1991). "The difference now is the quantity of violent events per hour and the special effects that make them seem all the more real."

To support their belief that this has a serious impact on young viewers, the Institute cites the following examples:

- A six-year-old boy wearing a turtle costume stabbed a friend in the arm for not returning a borrowed toy.

- A three-year-old boy picked up the family cat and swung it around his head like a Turtle hero wielding a weapon. When his mother tried to intervene, the boy said, "It's just like Michaelangelo."
- Two girls, aged four and five, were caught trying to climb down manholes to visit the Turtles' underground home.

Preschool teachers and day-care staffs in all provinces of Canada agree on the negative influence of the Turtles. "I hate the Turtles," says Carolyne Brennan, a teacher at a Toronto preschool. "One kid will kick another for no reason at all, and they don't relate the kicking with hurting. There's no question the Turtles incite kids to more violent behavior."

Because of that belief, Ms. Brennan bans toys and playground activities based on Ninja Turtles. She has also joined other professionals in a nationwide effort to reduce their influence.

Trying to do something about violence in the media raises the difficult issue of artistic freedom and censorship. That is not an issue that is easily solved in Canada or the United States, but before we delve into it, perhaps we ought to look at a few facts. In 1991 when the film "Boyz N the Hood" opened nationwide, incidents of violence followed:

- In a Chicago suburb, a man was fatally shot after a midnight showing.
- Five people were wounded in or near a large theater complex in Universal City, California.
- In Sacramento, a nineteen-year-old woman was shot six times during a fight outside a theater.
- In Tuscaloosa, Alabama, three teens were shot in a gang fight at a theater.

- In Commack, New York, a teenager was stabbed by two attackers in the lobby of a theater.

Some rock concerts seem to have a similar influence. Incidents of violence following attendance at a concert date back to the early 1980s. People were shot, stabbed, raped during the concerts or afterward, and sometimes gangs formed and roamed through cities attacking people and vandalizing property.

More recently, heavy metal groups such as Guns N Roses have had appearances canceled because of the incidence of violence. Security guards say it is increasingly hard to control violence during and after concerts.

A new twist in "entertainment" is making your own video. In December 1991 in the borough of Queens, New York, a nineteen-year-old attacked a sixteen-year-old, beat him, and ripped a gold chain from his neck, while an accomplice videotaped the whole event. According to Bob Greene of the *Chicago Tribune*, the incident is particularly frightening because some kids are acting out what they see on MTV—except that it isn't acting; it's for real.

Greene makes the point that ". . . music videos—specifically certain videos for rap music—are purposefully glorifying armed violence and criminality." Greene is concerned for the message that is given to young people through these videos. Are gunfights and street assaults the acceptable way to get what we want or settle our differences?

Some people argue that violence has been a part of entertainment since the days of early Greece. If it is so bad for us, someone would have proved it a long time ago and stopped it then. Why is it suddenly a big issue now?

According to Rollo May, a leading psychologist and author, the difference between violence in the classics and violence in modern entertainment is its purpose. Is it there just for the shock value, or is it an integral part of the story?

May suggests that the violence in the classics did serve a purpose. "After seeing a tragedy on stage or reading one, we often find ourselves wanting to walk by ourselves and think about it. We experience what Aristotle called the catharsis of pity and terror, and we long to savor it. It not only brings us closer to our own center, but also makes us more appreciative of our fellow men."

What that means is that we're not intended simply to accept violence as a way of life. We're supposed to question what it means to us and the people around us. Realizing what some people are capable of should make us more aware of the wrongness of it. It is part of the process of setting our own code of conduct that tells us we shouldn't or wouldn't do the same thing.

As an example, psychologist Margaret Singh cited the subtle influence of many of the TV detective shows. In her opinion, even the shows that don't glorify violence still do a disservice. She talked about an episode of "Columbo" in which two men conspired to kill their uncle for his money. "There was no sense of outrage over the crime," she said. "No sense of pathos over the victim. There is so much that isn't stated in shows like that that people absorb. What are they learning? That if you want your uncle's money, do him in. Just be clever enough not to get caught."

Along with the question of what purpose violence serves in film and television goes the issue of how much violence has to be shown and in how much detail.

We have always had a fascination with murder and murderers, especially the bizarre. What is new today is the detailed descriptions of those acts of murder. People no longer simply die in movies, they die with vivid eruptions of blood filmed so artistically that they have a perverse appeal.

An article in *Newsweek* (April 1991) suggests that violence in entertainment has gotten out of control and expresses a concern for what imaginary violence might be contributing to an increasingly dangerous real life. "Our ability to feel compassion is brutalized by excessive brutality, especially when it's given that Hollywood sheen." It is acknowledged that violence in stories is nothing new, but the point is made that the violence has become increasingly graphic and gory. This is true in books, television, and films. "What was considered daring filmmaking with 'Bonnie and Clyde' two decades ago is tame next to the gore in 'Die Hard II' and 'Robo Cop II'."

The graphic violence we see on screen is not always just a figment of someone's imagination. Since the mid-'60s when the Vietnam War was fought in living rooms across the nation on the evening news, broadcast journalism has become more and more daring. It no longer just tells us that someone was shot, with a discreet image hovering in the background. It shows us the bullet holes, the splattered blood, and creates a sense of drama out of real life.

Columnist Peter Riga, who is also a lawyer and a former professor of law and theology, believes that this brand of journalism promotes terrorism and other acts of violence. In a column (October 28, 1991), Riga makes some interesting points about the correlation between massacres and media coverage.

First, he states that the frequency of mass murders has increased dramatically in recent years. "From 1982 through 1986 there has been a massacre every year, and from 1987 to 1991 there have been two massacres a year with the exception of 1988."

Riga believes that the "meticulous and instant reporting of these massacres by the mass media" shares the responsibility for the increase in incidence. "Before TV, massacres were very infrequent. This is a horrible dilemma for the media, but the press needs to tone down the reportage of massacres, like terrorism, so as to lessen the trigger waiting to go off somewhere."

Some people still maintain that the violence we see and hear has no effect on us. In that way the producers need not accept responsibility. But two psychologists from the University of Illinois believe we cannot ignore the impact. Leonard Eron and L. Rowell Huesmann conducted a twenty-year study that found that kids who watched a great deal of TV violence at the age of eight were consistently more likely to commit violent crimes or abuse at age thirty. "We believe . . . that heavy exposure to televised violence is one of the causes of aggressive behavior, crime and violence in society," they wrote in 1984. "Television violence affects youngsters of all ages, of both genders, at all socioeconomic levels. . . . It cannot be denied or explained away."

Matthew Delapair, research coordinator for the National Coalition on TV Violence, asserts that watching TV violence has a detrimental effect on children. One effect is a "desensitization to watching violence and sexually degrading behavior," which is then taken into real life. Referring to studies from the U.S. Attorney General's task force on family, Delapair says that ". . . viewing violence helps foster the belief in children that such behavior is normal and acceptable."

More recently, a 1992 report by the American Psychological Association cited similar results. Dealing with a broad range of effects television has had on society, the report concluded that constant portrayal of sexual violence "leads to increased acceptance of rape" and "can instigate antisocial values and behavior."

Professor Haley, who has had years of experience in criminal justice, agrees. "We've destroyed our culture. Every time we entertain something destructive, we take another chink out of society."

He goes on to explain that our criminal justice system is based on Judeo-Christian values. Even people who are not followers of either faith could still believe in the values. But film and television attack those values. Too often they promote disrespect, lack of tolerance, cruelty, and greed.

"I can't imagine how hard it is for kids to watch TV and know how to live their lives," Professor Haley says. "They think that [what they see] is the acceptable way to respond to the same situation in real life. And there's very little influence out there telling them any different."

Some facts to back up those opinions were published in the *Journal of the American Medical Association* (June 10, 1992). In a study conducted in the United States, Canada, and South Africa, a direct correlation was found between television viewing and homicide. Between 1955 and 1975, as U.S. television ownership rose to nearly 100 percent of households, the homicide rate per 100,000 population rose from below 100 to 225. In Canada, the homicide rate rose from below 100 to just over 200. In both cases, the rise in TV ownership and the rise in homicides were almost perfectly matched. In white South Africa, where television was banned before 1975, the homicide rate grew by 130 percent from 1975 to 1987.

The study concludes that we as a society are conditioned by what we see as acceptable behavior. The problem is that most of us are not aware of the subtle influences.

TEENAGE OPINIONS

In an informal discussion group of five high school students, most agreed that we can be influenced by the
violence we see. But they didn't think watching "Friday
the 13th" would cause everybody to become violent. "It
can fuel violence," Paul said, "for kids who already have a
tendency to do it."

"Yeah, people who are real unstable might be more
influenced," Katie said. "Or if they're doing drugs or
something. But watching 'Die Hard' or 'The Terminator'
isn't going to make me go out and start killing people."

Okay. Watching those movies doesn't make you act
violently, but doesn't it affect you? What about being so
accustomed to seeing violence that you become desensitized—it becomes so much a part of your life that you
can't separate it from reality, and somehow that makes it
more acceptable?

"I don't think that's true," Matt said. "Everyone knows
it's just entertainment. They watch it for the thrills and
that's the end of it."

Kris didn't agree. "The gang movies are really bad," he
said. "They sort of glorify what goes on in real life. Direc-
tors and writers should be more responsible about how
they depict gangs and dope dealers and stuff like that."

Kris also believed there is a big difference between
those films and horror films like "Friday the 13th" or
"Texas Chainsaw Massacre." "You know they're fantasy,"
he said. "They're so exaggerated there's no way they're
going to get confused with real life. And people have been
watching horror films forever . . ."

Yes, but they didn't show the blood and guts in such
vivid detail. Do you think it's good to keep showing that
over and over?

"But that's the thrill of it," Matt said. "That's what kids want to see . . .

But where does responsibility come in? Do we keep giving kids what they want even when we suspect it might not be good for them?

"I don't think we should," Danielle said. "Most of it's pretty disgusting. And what purpose does it serve?"

"But that's censorship," Matt said. "What about—what is it—artistic freedom?"

Kris laughed. "They're not making these films and videos for artistic expression. They do it to make a lot of money."

The final consensus of the group was that entertainers and producers should use better judgment but should not be regulated by government. They also thought the rating system ought to be enforced more effectively. Too many children get in to see R-rated films. It was suggested that some sort of warning be given on TV when new films are being advertised.

A BETTER WAY

Childhood used to be a time of innocence. Children grew up protected from certain adult situations and information that they were considered not ready to handle. Some people still think that was a better way than feeding an ever-growing appetite for shocking entertainment and titillating information.

Columnist Ann Melvin in the *Dallas Morning News* made the following observation, "I think childhood now ends as soon as children can understand TV. Rock groups and rap bands sing songs about things adults used to go out on the porch to tell each other about. Today's aunts do not whisper in the kitchen about some family misconduct, they go on 'Oprah.' Every tragedy, every crime, is reported in grim and grisly detail, reenacted on TV, and if you still don't have the picture, there are diagrams."

In another column, Melvin wrote in reference to films like "Silence of the Lambs": "When the best talent in directing, cinematography and acting are used to make huge profits off the debasement of women and the portrayal of the occasional subhuman, violent male as fascinating— and the population as a whole is scammed into accepting this as entertainment—then we are in trouble."

To make her point on how damaging such films can be to children, she posed the question of how they will come to view the world. "Do they grow up thinking, 'Mother loves me. Her fried chicken smells great. Isn't it funny dandelions are a weed when they look so pretty in the spring sunshine. I wonder if the new kid at school will notice me in my new blue shirt.'?

"Or do they grow up terrorized of the dark, afraid of strangers, and more afraid of their own normal adolescent stirrings, certain that they foreshadow dark and troubling, yet inevitable, sexual encounters involving perversity, drugs and violence?"

At the end of that column, Melvin appealed to readers not to allow the trend to continue. She suggested that we walk out of such movies, that we write letters of protest to the theaters, production companies, TV stations, and advertisers.

Of course if we do that, we risk being laughed at. Some of our friends may give us a hard time, telling us to get real. But consider all the facts and decide which is the greater risk.

Looking at the influence of entertainment from another angle, columnist Bob Greene of the *Chicago Tribune* commented on the effects of the new craze for rap songs.

"What you have to understand is that for many young people, the rap videos are as glamorous a medium as there is. If gunfights and street assaults and robbery are legitimized in the videos—if they are excused as only the natural reaction to poverty and hopelessness—that is not a message that is lost on some viewers."

On a related subject, columnist Jeff Greenfield asked his readers to consider the impact of the comedy of Andrew Dice Clay: ". . . hateful speech, repellent speech, speech that stirs anger aimed at women, immigrants, gays, whomever. Unlike the material of Lenny Bruce or Richard Pryor, it illuminates nothing, satirizes nothing. It is a warm-up act for a Nuremberg rally." He concluded, "I also believe that those who produce contemptible expression—whether a comedian, a rap group, a flag burner or a major Hollywood studio—should be roundly, loudly condemned for debasing the culture by appealing to the worst within us."

Several other points are worth thinking about. The crime of rape is increasing at four times the rate of other crimes, and the incidence of rape in films is also increasing.

A recent study found that more preteens can identify the sadistic monsters of movies than can recognize George Washington, Abraham Lincoln, or Martin Luther King. To think such trends are unrelated to the growing number of rapes is to be naive.

Only time will tell whether these observers are being too reactionary. Much of the most graphic and shocking violence is so new that there has not been time to study the effects and draw conclusions. But concern is growing.

So, you may ask, "What does that have to do with me? I haven't bashed anybody lately because of a movie."

Maybe you'd like to take stock of your own tastes in movies, music videos, and TV programs. Ask yourself why you prefer what you do. What do you gain beyond a brief moment of entertainment? Is it worth it, knowing that such entertainment could be slowly eroding our society?

At some time in the future you might be more seriously affected. You might become a victim of the violence you take so lightly now. Or you might be looking at the situation through the eyes of a parent, wishing there was still a time of innocence for your children.

CHAPTER 7

The Leader of the Gang

Gangs arose in America in the middle 1800s, mostly in New York and Boston. As families immigrated to the United States, the young people banded together seeking a sense of identity and security. Most of them were Irish, but the idea of banding together appealed to other ethnic groups as well.

In those early years, gangs were not necessarily negative or violent. They merely satisfied a basic need by offering members a place to gather and belong. Many of the gangs were no different from a bunch of kids hanging out in a pizza place today. They just wanted to be around friends with whom they felt comfortable.

When the gangs began to experience harassment from other ethnic groups, the focus changed. Their instinctive response was to strike back, so a new element was added to their purpose—protection.

This ethnic protection is still a part of gang mentality

today. Black gangs fight Hispanic gangs in New York and Houston. White gangs fight Cuban gangs in Miami, and Asian gangs are attacked in Los Angeles. Each group considers itself superior to all others and is ready to shoot to prove it.

Criminal activity became part of gang operation in the 20th century, and with it came more violence. Now, with the widespread use of drugs and the availability of weapons, there is even more violence in gang activity.

According to sociologist Carl S. Taylor, who conducted a five-year study of gangs in Detroit, gangs are of three types.

Scavenger gangs are the least organized, and leadership changes frequently. Their crimes are usually not planned, and members are likely to be low achievers and dropouts. Scavenger gangs are looked down upon by other gangs.

Territorial gangs are turf-loyal groups and highly organized. They have initiation rites and other practices that separate members from nonmembers, and loyalty is obligatory.

The gang rituals practiced are very similar to those of adult clubs and social groups. Youth gangs adopt a cloak of secrecy not unlike some fraternities and wear similarly distinctive clothing or colors. Initiation rituals are also common to both groups. Prospective members have to prove their loyalty to the group. For the sorority "pledge" it might require something silly and harmless like running across campus in her underwear. For a youth gang "wannabee" it might mean something as serious and deadly as participating in a drive-by shooting.

The major activity of territorial gangs is fighting. As Taylor says, "The whole point of marking off your own territory is to keep somebody else out."

Some territorial gangs sell drugs; others don't. But the main purpose of the gang is still social, not economic.

Corporate gangs are highly structured criminal conspiracies organized to sell drugs. They can be compared to the "Mafia" gangs that sold liquor during Prohibition. Teens as young as fourteen are members of corporate gangs, although leadership is usually a few years older. These gangs operate under a strict code of behavior, and punishment for breaking the code is swift and severe. A corporate gang exists for the sole purpose of making money. The leaders must be capable of sophisticated strategic planning, personnel management, and financial management.

All three types of gangs operate independently of each other. Sometimes individuals move up from a territorial gang to a corporate gang, but most do not. Generally, it seems to be enough to be "somebody" within their own group.

Taylor did his study in the early '80s, before the influx of crack cocaine started influencing the gangs. That phenomenon brought a new element to the territorial gang. No longer were they as harmless as the Jets and the Sharks in "West Side Story."

The real gangs those fictional gangs were patterned after operated within a certain code of conduct. Random violence was limited, and gang business was kept within strict boundaries. "In the '50s and '60s fighting gangs were not involved in serious crime," says Sgt. John Galea, a twenty-year veteran of the New York City police gang unit. "Attacks on adults or families were off limits."

Even though their code was often outside the law, it still offered some protection to the general public. Today there is no code. Crack gangs are totally unpredictable and will do anything to make money. Many of the members come from violent backgrounds.

A study done in Philadelphia showed that most gang leaders were desensitized to violence by having been victims themselves. In their minds, violence was the only way to resolve disputes, the only response to criticism or rebuke. They simply knew no other way.

Most crack gangs range in size from six to thirty members, in their teens or twenties. Each gang tries to control a specific area, and many of them take over entire neighborhoods. Thousands of innocent people have died because they were in the wrong place during a gun battle between rival gangs. Others became victims of drive-by shootings.

By far the most violent crack gangs are Jamaican, and most of them are corporate gangs. Known as Posses, the Jamaican gangs were linked to more than 800 murders in the U.S. from 1985 to 1989. Thomas Moyer, an expert on the Posses, says they try to intimidate everyone, with little regard for human life. They brutalize members who try to hold back money or cheat the gang in any other way.

Many big-city crack gangs have expanded beyond their home base. Los Angeles gangs have moved into the Midwest to Kansas City and St. Louis and north to Seattle. Miami gangs have gone as far north as Atlanta and Savannah.

V.G. Guinses, director of a California agency that works to reduce the level of gang violence, compares this gang movement to ". . . franchising. They have decided to do what the Kentucky Colonel and McDonald's have done."

The approach to a new city is well organized and businesslike. The dealers pass out free samples and offer the product for less than the competition. They break from business tradition in that they intimidate the competition with violence and murder.

Al Santoli, in an article in *PARADE* magazine (March 24, 1991), reports on the phenomenal growth of youth gangs since the mid-1980s. "Boston with six known gangs in 1987, now has twenty-five with 650 members. Between 1984 and 1988, Miami's four gangs grew to sixty with more than 3,000 members. The Seattle area claims fifty gangs, mostly new. Milwaukee reports 4,000 gang members. Denver has 3,000 and Phoenix has 2,000." Santoli also notes that while the size of gangs and number of members are rising, the age of members is dropping. In 1984 most gang members were fifteen; today, the average age is thirteen and a half.

Los Angeles County has about 1,000 gangs with a total membership of 150,000. It has been considered the gang capital of the country because of the size of gangs as well as their involvement in violent crime.

In April 1992 the city of Los Angeles erupted in a terrible riot following the acquittal of four white police officers who were on trial for beating a black man, Rodney King. Gang members joined other citizens in venting their anger and frustration by burning and looting a large section of South Central Los Angeles.

Los Angeles County District Attorney Ira Reiner said that gangs did not start the riots but certainly participated. Early in June, twenty-two suspected members of a West Los Angeles gang were arrested on charges of looting $80,000 worth of high-tech equipment from a Korean-owned stereo store. Gang members were also charged in the near-fatal beating of a truck driver in the first days of the riot.

In the aftermath of the riot, two of the major gangs, the Crips and the Bloods, called for a truce. Initially, the truce was suspect because it was thought to be an effort to focus gang fury on police officers. After six weeks of relative peace, however, there were no attacks on police, nor were there any gang-related homicides. "They [the gangs] are not coming together to organize against law enforcement," said one community gang worker. "They're coming together for mere survival because they have been to too many funerals."

A major reason so many of the gangs survive despite the dangers is that young kids simply see no other choice. One sixteen-year-old member of a Chicano gang in South Central Los Angeles told a *Time* reporter, "I was born and raised in South Central, and gangs are all that I see. That's the only alternative I've got, and I have to take what comes. It's pitiful. A lot of people die, and it keeps going on. But it's like a ball rolling and rolling. There's no solution to it. There are just always going to be gangs."

GROUP THINK

For some people, belonging to a gang can make violent acts more acceptable. Gang members can channel the guilt and responsibility to the group as a whole.

This transference of guilt is similar to what happens in wartime. Soldiers give over their moral responsibility to the unit and the superiors. Under other circumstances, normal men and women do not carry assault rifles and seek out their enemies to kill them. In war, however, it is the natural thing to do. Soldiers need not feel morally responsible for their actions because they are under orders. Someone else has the responsibility for putting them where they are and telling them what to do.

It is this same transference of responsibility that can open the door to acts of cruelty and violence beyond the call of duty. The massacre at Mylai during the Vietnam War is an example, but it is not unique. Every war has had its dark moments when soldiers lost control and killed innocent people.

According to Rollo May, a phenomenon of war experience is what leads some soldiers past a certain point. It erodes individual responsibility and conscience. Men have given over their freedom of choice to the group and find it difficult to get it back when they need it.

That same personal erosion of responsibility occurs in gang violence as well. In some gangs, the violence is controlled by the leader, who is strong enough to dictate whether and when force will be used. Less organized gangs are more haphazard in their violence. Sometimes they are more brutal because they can be dominated by their most hateful and daring members.

In either case, the outcome can be the same. "When young males come together as a gang, the group exerts a powerful influence that is capable of eliciting violent, illegal, and antisocial acts from individual members that they would not necessarily commit if acting alone," says Dr. Deborah Prothrow-Stith, public health official and author. "In the context of the gang, vile acts may be committed by adolescents who in themselves appear to be rather ordinary."

Teens are especially susceptible because they are so sensitive to peer pressure. They need the affirmation of bonding with a group, even if that group is destructive. Then they are often challenged to go along with group plans, even when they would rather not.

Frank Zimring, director of the Earl Warren Legal Institute at the University of California, believes that violent teen groups are run by "government by dare—you do it because you don't want to back out."

There's no doubt that gang activity has changed from the turf wars and street fighting of years past. Now it involves sophisticated weaponry, drug money, and random killings.

In Los Angeles County, street gang killings are up by nearly 25 percent, to the highest level in six years. Gang members were responsible for 690 killings and 6,278 assaults with a deadly weapon. Those, however, were only the ones reported. There's no way to measure those that go unnoticed except by the victims.

Dennis Anderson, in an article in the Los Angeles *Star Tribune* (March 7, 1987), made the statistics more personal:

"Essie Love, a social worker from Watts, shudders every time she see yellow ribbons in her neighborhood. Police string up the yellow bands to rope off homicide scenes. In the troubled turf where she lives and works, the victims too often are children killed in gang-related violence.

" 'The parents lose one child to the gangs and grieve. We counselors lose a child every week,' the veteran counselor for Community Youth Gang Services said. 'Sometimes it's almost too much to bear.' "

Several factors contribute to the rise in gang activity and gang violence in our schools and streets. One primary contributor is the widespread use of drugs. Even if gang members are not into dealing, many of them are users, and the drug of choice has become crack cocaine.

Unlike marijuana and alcohol, the other two most popular drugs, crack is a stimulant. It makes users jumpy and irritable. Sometimes it even makes them paranoid, and they imagine threats all around them. Their response to that imagined threat is violence.

The breakdown of the family unit is also a strong contributor to the rise in gang membership. People of any age need a place to belong, a place that gives them personal security. That is especially true when you're young. If you do not find that place at home, you feel lost and powerless.

Let's look for a moment at power and the need for power. Like aggression, the word power is often misunderstood. The word comes from the Latin *posse*, "to be able." We need power literally to be able to do the things we need to do. Without power, we cannot accomplish goals or rise to new levels of achievement. That is why powerlessness is such a strong motivator.

A great deal of what happens between people is a conflict between power and powerlessness. People who are oppressed for any reason feel helpless and weak—not able. Out of that powerlessness come frustration, anger, and often violence.

In *Power and Innocence*, Rollo May writes, "Deeds of violence in our society are performed largely by those trying to establish their self-esteem, to defend their self-image, and to demonstrate that they, too, are significant."

If you think perhaps May is exaggerating, remember what you wanted to do the last time you were frustrated and angry. Maybe you wanted to hit your dad when he thoughtlessly put you down. Or whack your little brother when he called you a nerd. Or deck your best friend when he teased you about getting dumped by your girlfriend.

All of those inclinations are responses to a need to defend yourself and your self-image.

Rollo May also says, "A person on a binge of violence becomes unfeeling and detached, like a soldier mowing down the enemy with a machine gun. Or else he could never do what he feels he has to do."

WHAT CAN WE DO?

If we don't find a way to eliminate the need for gangs, the problems of violence will continue to sweep the country.

That is a major concern for school administrators, counselors, law-enforcement personnel, and others. What is important is that many of them are responding. Not all responses are effective, as we shall see in Chapter 9, but some are. And government is beginning to listen to those who know best.

In 1988, the U.S. House of Representatives appointed a Select Committee to examine the problems of children, youth, and families. Marianne Diaz-Parton, who works with Community Youth Gang Services of Los Angeles, testified before the committee on March 9, 1988. She stated her belief that groups like hers offer the best hope for reaching gang members. Her organization employs streetwise counselors, some of them former gang members who can talk from experience and show kids that there is a better way out of their circumstances.

She suggested that, ". . . schools hire people who are capable of counseling youth involved in gangs, counseling the teachers, counseling the parents, and bringing people to understand that giving up on these kids is giving up on the future."

Some programs being formed to help with the problem of gangs and violence are discussed in Chapter 11. The group dynamics that work so well in the street gangs **can** be turned around to something positive. It works especially well when very young teens and preteens are offered alternatives before they are drawn into a gang.

As we have seen, young people join gangs for a variety of reasons: to have a place to belong, to be accepted, to be noticed—and sometimes just to have something to do.

Many other organizations can meet those needs without leading you into a destructive life-style. You probably didn't join the drama club or the German club with a conscious awareness that it gave you a place to belong and be accepted. You did it because it looked like fun. Once you were in, you wanted to participate because it made you feel good to be part of the group. It also made you feel good to be noticed and appreciated for things you did for the group. Feeling good made you more eager to do more things, but you never thought about the group dynamics.

Not everyone has an opportunity to join such a group, however. Many of the inner-city schools have little to offer the students as alternatives to street gangs, and even what is offered has limited appeal. It's not considered "cool" to join the pep club.

To combat that problem, teachers at T.J. Rusk Middle School in Dallas started the Good Guys Gangs. In some ways they operate like any other gang: They meet regularly; they have secret signs and codes of greeting; and they attempt to wear similar clothing so they can be easily recognized.

Where they differ from other gangs is their purpose. In an area where street gangs are such a strong influence, members of the Good Guys Gangs try to help each other resist that influence.

It seems like such a little thing, it's hard to imagine it will have much effect on the whole problem. But remember that all change starts with one or two little things. And if we do nothing, the aggressors will win.

CHAPTER 8

Violence on the Rise

"I find trying to survive in this world very hard, but when there's violence on the streets, it makes survival even harder. I think about how many innocent people get killed every day. I think about kids getting killed at young ages. I think about the elderly people who have no one to do things for them . . . I think about the fear that they have each time they come out of their homes . . .

. . . Tomorrow is another day. And I wonder what it will bring. But deep down inside I already know that it will be another day of trying to find a safe route home from school, seeing kids on the streets trying to be bad, seeing some old person walking in fear, seeing the police cars, with their lights flashing, and their sirens on, seeing the ambulance coming and going, and seeing the youth of America being shot down, and killed, before they even had a chance to live."

The above quotation is from an essay written by a seventeen-year-old student at Jeremiah E. Burke High

School in Boston. In 1989 Dr. Deborah Prothrow-Stith and her coauthor, Michaele Weissman, asked the students to write about their concerns about violence. Their essays were filled with fear, despair, and feelings of powerlessness.

Those feelings are created by a tough reality. A report by Dr. Wade F. Horn, Commissioner for Children, Youth and Families for the U.S. Department of Health and Human Services, notes that on an average day 135,000 children carry a gun to school.

Even though violence is one of the most discussed subjects today, it is not new to the American way of life. From the very beginning, disputes, large and small, have been settled by strength and firepower.

Abraham Lincoln spoke out against violence long before he became President. He called it the nation's major domestic problem and expressed concern for "the increasing disregard for law that pervades the country."

What is new about violence is that it is involving more and more young people.

Under the headline: MORE HOUSTON TEENS SHOOTING, GETTING SHOT, a recent newspaper story stated that teens are three times more likely to be wounded or shot to death than the average resident. They are also doing most of the shooting. In January 1992 alone, eleven Houston teens were killed and ten others arrested as murder suspects.

Dr. Paul Pepe, director of Houston's emergency services, said the number of teens wounded in shootings tripled in 1990 and predicted that the number in 1991 would be even higher. "This trend is reaching deeper and deeper into the heart of our youth."

Another new element in violence is what kids are being killed for. A certain logic can be argued in disputes over money, drugs, territory, and honor. But what about all the kids who are being killed for what they wear?

The problem is serious enough that some people are starting programs to help kids avoid being victims. Milwaukee has an organization called Parents and Youth Concerned About Fashion and Violence. Columnist Bob Greene of the Chicago *Tribune* interviewed the founder of the organization. "We're trying to educate the young people that if they wear certain things it may cost them their lives," said Irma Walker. "Basically, we're trying to teach them to dress smart. Don't wear anything that anyone else would want and would try to take from you."

Greene wondered if that approach was attacking the wrong problem. It seemed to him to blame the victims and potential victims, sending a despairing message to young people. "It probably is, but in the society in which we live, it's an important message," Ms. Walker said. "The truth is that our young people are in danger for what they wear. Just recently a boy here was shot in the chest and killed for his Chicago Bulls jacket."

On a national scale, arrests for homicides among juveniles has gone up 93 percent in the past four years. That compares to an increase of 16 percent among adult offenders in the same time period.

WHY THE ESCALATION?

The main question is why it has suddenly grown to almost epidemic proportions. Some of the reasons have been touched on in earlier chapters, but others are worth looking at.

Tristram Coffin, editor of *The Washington Spectator*, addressed the topic in an article (May 15, 1989). He attributed the upswing to four major factors: poverty, easy access to guns, drugs, and other social factors.

Poverty

Poverty has been creating social problems since the beginning of history. People who are poor feel oppressed, powerless, and resentful of people who are not poor. They live with the daily frustration of barely scraping by day after day. Often that frustration leads to anger and aggressive violence.

Perhaps the most damaging aspect of poverty is the lack of hope. Writing in the Milwaukee *Journal*, George Miller stated, "Children growing up in our poorest neighborhoods are far more likely to fare poorly in school, become teenage mothers, suffer chronic unemployment, and resort to crime and violence. They grow up with little investment in their future and little evidence from their bleak environment that the future is something worth investing in. When they pull a gun and risk a jail term, they have very little to risk."

That happens all too often in inner-city neighborhoods where poverty has been a way of life for generations. The children quickly learn that their lives are controlled by outside forces, and they no longer believe that they have any power to make it better. That lack of power often turns to frustration and rage.

Economic problems are no longer considered a factor only in poor neighborhoods. Unemployment is rising among middle-class Americans, and the sudden onset of financial difficulties increases their frustrations. This can lead to the same sense of hopelessness and powerlessness felt for generations by the poorer classes.

Availability

The availability of guns is a second factor in the rising rate of violence. In *Time* magazine (March 9, 1992), Lance

Morrow wrote, "Gun violence is spreading like AIDS."
Even beyond the kids' claim that they need a gun for
protection, guns have a certain allure, according to
Morrow. "Guns have a sort of irresistible black magic
about them. A good gun has such a lovely heft, a densely
sinister weight in the hand. The finger twitches . . . and
the life across a distance disintegrates. Guns have become
the neighborhood logic, rite of passage, administrator,
avenger, instrument of impulse and rough justice. They
are a symbol of manhood and power in a world that has
given the young neither self-discipline nor much to hope
for."

George Napper, Commissioner of the Department of
Public Safety in Atlanta, believes that as long as guns are
so easily available, the violence will continue to increase.
In testimony before a senate subcommittee in 1988, he
called for gun control:

"We in law enforcement are in a dilemma. We want to
make every street safe for walking or driving day or night.
We want to return the sounds of children playing ball . . .
to every park. We want to return every parking place
in apartments and housing complexes to the law-abiding
resident.

"We're making every effort to do just that. However, as
long as the potpourri of gun laws in this country allows
our agencies to be outnumbered and outgunned; and as
long as we continue to allow our officers to be at maximum
risk each day they're on the beat, we can not realistically
expect to win and provide you and all of our citizens the
total protection [they] deserve."

Perhaps you're still not convinced of the need for gun
control. If you're still trying to make up your mind, consider the following:

- The *Journal of the American Medical Association* published homicide rates for young men age fifteen to twenty-four in developed nations for the year 1986–1987. The United States had the highest rate, 21.9 per 100,000—between four and seventy-three times the rate in any other industrial nation.
- Researchers did a comparative study of the homicide rates of Seattle and Vancouver, British Columbia, cities only 140 miles apart and similar in size, income levels, and unemployment rates. From 1980 to 1986, Seattle had 388 homicides; Vancouver, 204. In both cities the overall number of deaths was about the same; what was different was the deaths by shooting. In Seattle where handguns are easily available, 139 people were killed by bullets. In Vancouver, which has restrictive handgun laws, the deaths by shooting numbered 25.

At some point, we are going to have to recognize that guns **are** killing people.

Drugs

Drugs also play a significant role in the rise of violence. As we saw in the previous chapter, many gangs are involved in drugs, and disputes over money and territory lead to violence.

Drugs are also a leading cause of crime outside of gang activity. According to James Stewart, Director of the National Institute of Justice, people who use one of the major illegal drugs commit four to six times as many crimes as nondrug users.

Nearly half of the juveniles in correctional institutions in 1987 for violent crimes were under the influence of drugs or alcohol when they committed their offenses. The leading causes of death among teenagers and young adults—unintentional injuries, suicide, and homicide— are in many cases linked to drug abuse.

The drug business also brings violence to young people who are not users and are not gang members.

In *The Dream Sellers*, Richard H. Blum writes about the drug business in Oakland, California. Kids as young as six or seven can start to develop a reputation for being "bad" by drinking, smoking, and sniffing glue.

If they're "bad" enough by the time they are nine or ten, they can get a job as a lookout for a drug dealer, making as much as $100 a day by warning when the police are in the area.

To get such a job, and more important, to keep it, the kids have to add fighting to their reputation. That is part of the total image they want to develop. "You've got to be a rough little dude when you're coming up," one boy said. "You got to be tough to survive."

The next step for young teens in the drug business is being a runner, for which they make $300 a day. After proving themselves as runners, some teens move into dealing. By then, they've established their "tough guy" image and proved they can handle any situation. Young dealers can make as much as $3,000 a day in large cities.

The money to be had in the drug business has a tremendous appeal, especially for inner-city kids who often see no other way out of poverty. But money is not all the kids get.

What many of them fail to realize is the personal danger involved in the business. They already consider themselves invincible by their survival up to this point, and the danger always exists for "someone else." Someone else will die if a deal goes bad. Someone else will die in a dispute over territory. Someone else will die in a drug raid.

In *Violence and Drugs*, Gilda Berger writes that authorities report increasingly brutal and bizarre crimes commited by young dealers. She cites incidents in Detroit where boys as young as fourteen have been arrested for torture—inflicting powerful electric shocks, and pouring alcohol on open wounds.

A cause-and-effect relationship between violence and the use of drugs is hard to establish, according to Berger. Some experts doubt that criminals commit more crime when they are on drugs; others believe it is the need for money to buy drugs that leads to crime, not the drugs themselves.

"Most drugs are depressants, so they wouldn't cause violence," says psychologist Gyoengyver Soggin, who has years of experience in drug rehab centers. "But they do lower impulse control, so the potential for violence is there."

The exception, however, is crack, which has been proved to cause violence. A tragic example is an incident that happened in New York in 1988. A seventeen-year-old crack addict robbed and shot five people in a six-hour period one day. The next day he robbed three stores, shooting five more people. After two more days of violence, the police finally caught the boy, ending what was considered the worst juvenile crime spree in the city's history.

Another factor in the connection of drug use and violence is decreased inhibitions. People on drugs are more apt to participate in violent acts because they feel no sense of involvement in what they are doing. People who use drugs daily have a constant cloud over their reality, which often includes violence.

In interviews with comedian Paul Rodreguiz on a special entitled "Back to School" (Feb. 16, 1992), teens talked freely about some of the problems they face, including drugs. Most said they had started using drugs at age eleven. One girl said she didn't like it that much, but she kept doing it because she was looking for a feeling. Another girl said that when you do drugs you belong to a culture; you have friends you feel comfortable with and know you're accepted.

Another girl started with drugs at age eleven and crashed at fifteen; now at seventeen she is trying to put her life back together. She said, "Whatever it is you're using drugs to avoid, you can probably live through it. Whatever drugs you are taking will probably kill you. If they don't kill you now, they'll kill you tomorrow. And the time in between will be just unbearable."

It is easy to see the connection between poverty, guns, drugs, and violence. It is also natural to point a finger at those causes and think if we could only get rid of them, the violence would stop.

Eliminating poverty, guns, and drugs would help, but it wouldn't make the problem go away. There are too many other negative influences that we have to eliminate before we can see a change.

CHAPTER 9

Creating Violence

"A culture is shaped, a civilization endures, not by immediate cause and effect, buy by persevering dedication to
what is most advantageous to it—and by outrage at that
which threatens to destroy what is most valuable in it."
                                    —Columnist Ann Melvin

Many experts believe that the foundation of
violent behavior starts long before the
fourteen-year-old picks up a gun and shoots
somebody. An accumulation of social influences are at
work over a period of time before the problem becomes
a newspaper headline.

The most crucial influence is the family. According
to Dr. Prothrow-Stith, "Violence is a problem that
begins at home."

She believes that parents can teach their kids how
to function in a social setting without bashing those
who stand in their way. But the parents have to *be*
there for that to happen, and too many parents aren't.

For a variety of reasons, more and more children
today are growing up in single-family homes or homes

where both parents work. In some cases there is no harmful effect. The kids still feel loved and nurtured. There is adequate supervision.

In other cases, however, the kids are virtually on their own for long periods of time. They may feel lost and lonely, resenting the absence of their parents without even recognizing the feeling or why they have it. More important, they may never have the opportunity to learn from their parents all the lessons about right and wrong, responsibilities and consequences.

In a 1982 study at the Behavioral Research Institute, Rachelle Cantor discovered that teens who are deeply involved in family life rarely have problems of delinquency. Teens who come from divorced families have a much higher rate of delinquency.

Similarly, in a study of gangs, sociologist Francis Ianni reported that almost all the gang members came from broken or severely disturbed and deprived homes.

Another study showed that 72 percent of boys and girls in correctional institutions had grown up without one or both parents.

What these children miss in their lives goes far beyond the physical presence of parents. According to Dr. Prothrow-Stith, the most important thing kids get from their parents is a sense of being loved. "A child's capacity to feel love, to give love, and to mature into a responsible, participating adult requires the presence of loving adults who stay put year after year." She also believes that it is vital for children to have consistency, security, and discipline in their lives. They are hurt if their parents don't care enough to pay attention to them, and they are disappointed if standards are not set for them.

Paul Lauer, a youth minister and editor of *YOU* magazine, agrees. In an interview, he said it is not realistic to expect young people to do everything an adult says. On the other hand, it is important to inform them of the ideals and values that make for a better life. "They like to hear what we are asking and expecting them to strive for. That gives them a certain amount of dignity. It tells them that we expect a lot from them, but it also tells them we believe they can achieve those goals."

The isolation of the family unit has also seriously diminished its effectiveness. In years past, when whole families were born, lived, and died in the same neighborhood, the full responsibility of childraising did not rest only with the parents. Grandparents, aunts, uncles, and even the next-door neighbor got into the act. Kids couldn't go down the street or even a few blocks away to misbehave because someone was sure to see them and tell their parents.

But these "watchers" served another, vital role. They were people the kid could turn to with a problem when the parent wasn't around. They were people who could offer the kid a bit of wisdom and truth from a perspective that perhaps made it more acceptable than coming from a parent.

Our current, more transient society has removed that support from families. Parents have no one to back them up, and kids have no one to turn to when they need help or advice, or perhaps just someone to listen.

Kent Amos, who works with teens in Washington, D.C., calls this phenomenon the breakdown of the "tribal process." Amos was quoted extensively in a column by William Raspberry. "The problem with today's children is that the tribe is no longer functioning," Amos says. "Now, adult neighbors often don't know each other, let alone one another's children. Families are dispersed. There are no neighborhoods and communities as before."

Amos speaks of the *covenant* that once existed between

families, the neighborhood, the political leaders, and the church leaders, who all shared responsibility for teaching and nurturing young people. Everybody was involved and everyone cared, and the system worked.

Amos believes the system can still work, and does in certain areas. "If you go into the most drug-infested and violent neighborhood in the city, you'll find children who come through in reasonably good shape. Follow them back and you will find a covenant kind of environment, where families and neighbors work together to help bring the children up right. These kinds of environments exist all over the place. We need to hold them up, and do what we can to reinforce them."

Young People Speak

Clint, a twenty-one-year-old college student, agrees that the health and well-being of families is vital. "Because we have all these problems [dysfunctional families], our value system is falling apart," he says. "Kids no longer have a clear sense of right and wrong."

"There's no guidance," says Danielle, a seventeen-year-old high school student. "Kids are left on their own too much."

Most of the teens recognize a certain aimlessness in their friends who don't have strong family support. "They just sorta hang out with nothing to do," says Katie. "And no one to tell them they shouldn't do something stupid like get in a fight."

A good example of Katie's point is an incident in a suburban high school where several dozen kids were involved in a fight. "It was nothing but foolishness," a sixteen-year-old said. "I don't think anyone but one guy wanted to fight. The rest just got caught up in it."

Another student agreed. "I got there at 8:00 and everyone was getting along. By 8:15, it was wild."

The fight was sparked by bad feelings between a black student and a white student. According to the principal, things had been simmering between the two boys for a week before it erupted. The emotion of the moment just seemed to pull other kids into it, even though they had nothing against each other.

On the Other Hand

Some of the material in this chapter may make you think that everyone who comes from a troubled background is going to become a violent criminal or a gang member. Many of them do, but the circumstances don't predestine everyone. For every ten kids who follow the cycle of poverty and crime, one or two always pull themselves out and say, "No more. I don't have to do this just because everyone else is doing it."

A key factor in being able to do that is recognizing the freedom of choice, and exercising it. For some kids, like Tim in Chapter 1, the recognition comes pretty late, but it is better then never realizing it at all.

We also cannot overlook how difficult it is to pull out of the mire of poverty, hopelessness, and crime. Those who have never experienced it can only imagine the strength of character it takes.

DON'T JUST BLAME IT ON FAMILIES

An entire social system beyond the family influences young people as they are growing up. The community, the neighborhood, churches, schools, law enforcement, the media, and government all have their effects. To single out one element to blame makes no sense.

The problem of violence is complicated, and so is the influence of all these other factors. Professor Haley compares the rise in violence to a prairie fire: It starts in one place and just keeps spreading, gaining fuel and momentum as it goes.

Beyond the primary reasons, Professor Haley cites other causes of violence, some of which are tied to a breakup of values. "We used to have a common culture, a shared base of beliefs and values. Kids learned that at home, at school, and in the community. Now, we can't even agree on what is acceptable. There's nothing to pass on to our kids, so they haven't been taught that there are alternatives to the messages they get from popular belief.

"The loss of this value system has left too many kids without a clear distinction between right and wrong. Some of them even end up in court without realizing what they did was wrong."

Haley believes we started losing our value system about thirty years ago. The '60s were the age of "letting it all hang out" and the beginning of permissiveness in parenting. "If it feels good, it's okay," was a motto that spawned a lot of social problems, including a surge in crime.

"What we've done is carry that idea to the present," says Haley. "Now it's 'do only what you like.' School is not relevant unless it's interesting. Everything has to be fun or entertaining or some kids don't want any part of it."

Writing in the Milwaukee *Journal* (February 1984), Tom Boswell also expressed the thought that the rise in juvenile violence is a reflection of the breakdown of values. Youth gangs striving for money and accepting violence as a means of getting it are a by-product of our ambitious, self-serving society. The kids learn those lessons from the behavior of adults.

Another journalist, William Murchison, addressed the same topic. In his column (December 4, 1991), he wrote that a moral collapse is at the root of our crime problems. Referring to "moral sterility," he said that society is no longer bound by a moral consensus. "Ours is an age of relativism. Right and wrong are matters of taste and opinion. Usually right is what I want to do, whereas wrong is anything you do to stop me." Murchison concluded with a plea to start rebuilding a moral consensus, ". . . to pick up the shards and fragments of the commandments and precepts we broke so carelessly."

That is not a popular idea, nor is it be particularly easy. We have all grown accustomed to having our own way and living the philosophy of the '60s. But we can see the effect of that life-style all around us, and it isn't good.

PAYING OUR DUES

For a number of reasons, young people are not afraid of the consequences of their actions. Some of the fault for that lies in the lack of parental training, restrictions on what can be taught about values in school, and problems in the criminal justice system.

In her book *At a Tender Age*, Rita Kramer blames the juvenile courts for not punishing violent acts. She cites the legal definition of a "juvenile delinquent": a person "over seven and less than sixteen years of age, who, having committed an act that would constitute a crime if committed by an adult. . . . is not criminally responsible for such conduct by reason of infancy. . . . (Family Courts Act, 1983, Article 3, Part 1).

As an example of how misguided that law is, she gives

the case of a twelve-year-old offender who, with two other boys, had raped and beaten a bag lady in New York's Central Park. Because of his age, the boy was sentenced to eighteen months in a juvenile detention center.

Kramer finds fault with a system that treats a twelve-year-old with leniency for a serious violent offense, but will "close the book on him when he reaches the arbitrary age of sixteen, seventeen, or eighteen, turning him over to the 'adult' system."

Kramer believes that reforms to integrate the two systems are the best answer. Young people who commit crimes of extreme violence have to face more serious consequences.

Journalist Patrick Buchanan is in agreement. In an article in the *Conservative Chronicle* (May 10, 1989), he commented on "wilding" and "wolfpack" incidents and called for hard-line reactions. "Since legislation protecting the rights of juvenile offenders often leaves them without significant punishment, maybe it's time to redefine the offender and the consequence. . . . Historically, civilized nations have put an end to savagery by traditional means, instilling fear into the barbarians. . . . We are losing the war on crime because our troops are demoralized, and the enemy is unafraid."

Professor Haley has a more temperate view. He agrees that we need more accountability for young offenders, but he doesn't think putting them through the adult system works. "We create another problem in labeling juvenile offenders. They're tried in adult court and they get a permanent record, a label. They become 'a murderer'. For many of them, that becomes a self-fulfilling prophesy."

When the juvenile justice system started, the ideal was to have a judge who understood human behavior and the law. The reality, according to Professor Haley, does not begin to reach the ideal. There are problems of inexperience within the whole system, he points out. Some states have judges who hear adult cases all morning, then switch to juvenile cases in the afternoon. They have no training or experience to deal with the special needs of juvenile cases.

Haley believes that will continue to be a problem until the system is reformed, but he doesn't know when that will happen. "Special commissions have formed off and on for years to revamp the system, but very little effective change has come about."

Until that happens, Haley agrees with Rita Kramer that the criminal justice system will continue to affect the violence rate in America.

CHAPTER 10

Accepting the Consequences

On January 5, 1991, life took a dramatic turn for fifteen-year-old Todd. It wasn't the day he got his driving permit, or his first job, or a date with the girl he'd been dreaming about for weeks. No, this was the day he walked into a gas station with two other people and shot a man to death during an attempted robbery.

At the time, Todd was not a hardened criminal or a gang member. He was not even a street-wise kid who grew up in a tough neighborhood. He was just an ordinary guy from a suburban background who got mixed up with the wrong people.

At his trial, his mother testified that Todd seemed "like a scared little boy" when he told her about the shooting. "He said he just turned around and did it. He said he just stood there until he realized what he had done."

Police found Todd still standing there looking at the

body. He was arrested at the scene, indicted for capital murder, and certified to stand trial as an adult.

Todd went to trial in June, was found guilty, and was sentenced to life in prison. The prosecutor considered the sentence appropriate, even for a fifteen-year-old. "If you do adult crimes, you should suffer adult punishments," he said.

That same month, three other teens were arrested and charged with a racially motivated murder. They had driven by where a young black man was drinking beer with a couple of white friends after work, and shot him.

The three were traced to their homes, where police found white supremacist literature. All of them were heavily tattooed with racist slogans.

Because of the seriousness of the crime, the teens were tried as adults. The one who had pulled the trigger of the shotgun was sentenced to life in prison; the other two received lesser terms.

In March 1991, a seventeen-year-old was arrested and charged with murder. But he had not killed a stranger. He killed his mother, dumped her body, and began using her credit cards.

He, too, was convicted of capital murder.

What these cases have in common is the relative youth of the participants and the end result. All are now serving time in prison.

After the conviction, Todd's attorney told reporters that he hoped his client would not have to spend the rest of his life in prison. "My hope is that he'll use his time in the penitentiary system wisely, get an education, maybe get a job skill, and turn it all around."

That could be a satisfactory conclusion to the story if we could believe that Todd would learn all the right stuff in the next ten years or so. Then he could be paroled, return to society, and lead a productive life. But the chances of that are slim.

What is more likely is that Todd will be intimidated, brutalized, beaten, used by other inmates. His only option will be to work within the system—not the government-controlled system, but the power structure operated by the inmates.

Todd will learn to be stronger, meaner, and more powerful than the guy next to him. He will learn how to pull jobs without getting caught, and how to handle killing without standing there looking at the body until the police show up. That's the "education" Todd is likely to acquire in prison.

The situation is not much better for those who go to Juvenile Detention Centers Maximum. Professor Haley describes one such place in northern Ohio called Indian River. "The young offenders go there until they turn 21. There's no parole or early release or time off for good behavior, so they don't care about obeying the rules. It's one of the toughest places to be, no matter which side of the law you're on."

A LOOK AT THE SYSTEM

Charles Silberman, in *Criminal Violence—Criminal Justice*, writes that violent crime will not be eliminated until every person in America becomes a full participating member of society with a major stake in its preservation. But he also believes that we cannot minimize the impact of the criminal justice system.

Some people consider it the "Band-Aid" approach, covering up the sore without healing it. But Silberman says, "Even Band-Aids have their purpose. No competent or compassionate doctor would leave a festering sore unbandaged or fail to treat some other painful symptom, especially if a cure was not immediately at hand."

The criminal justice system is made up of three parts: law enforcement, the judiciary, and the penal system.

Law enforcement can be considered the foot soldiers of the system: city police officers, county sheriffs, state marshals, and federal agents.

The judiciary begins at the county line and goes all the way up to the federal court system: civil courts, criminal courts, family courts, and some juvenile courts.

The penal system is just as vast and complicated as the court system. The federal prison system includes youth and juvenile institutions, young adult institutions, adult penitentiaries, adult correctional institutions, short-term camps, institutions for women, community treatment centers, and medical treatment centers.

Most of the inmates in federal institutions have been convicted of white-collar crimes. Fewer of them have committed crimes of violence than those in state prisons. Some criminologists believe the quality of the federal prisons is higher than that of prisons in most states.

State prison systems have most of the same types of institutions as the federal system, but each state operates independently. In one state you might be sent to prison for robbery, in another state to a halfway house or a detention center.

Below the state system are county and city jails, which are usually short-term facilities. Most of the prisoners are waiting for trial, serving time for misdemeanors, or waiting to be moved to a state facility.

Abuse of Authority

Each part of the criminal justice system has had its own problems and has received the blame for the overall ineffectiveness of the whole.

Some police officers abuse their authority. They operate outside the law they are sworn to uphold. They mistreat prisoners. And the general public says, "That's what's wrong with the system."

Some judges also abuse their authority, especially in juvenile courts. Silberman points out in his book that some judges make decisions that could not possibly reflect the best interests of the people involved. One such case involved a teenage girl who was petitioning to be released from a training center. Her probation officer and her parents agreed that the girl would do better to go to an alternative school and start working at a job that was already lined up. The judge decided she should stay in the training center because it offered a course in cosmetology. It didn't matter to him that she didn't want to do this, nor that those who knew her well did not consider it the best course.

People hear about incidents like that and say, "That's what's wrong with the justice system."

People who run the prisons and detention centers also abuse their authority. They do little or nothing to rehabilitate the prisoners, and they turn a blind eye to the inmates' power structure. At most of these institutions, prisoners are dehumanized and trained to be better criminals. And people say, "That's what's wrong with the justice system."

The responsibility for what's wrong with the system does not rest with any one branch. Every weak link in the chain is pulling the whole structure down.

A Day in the Life . . .

In most states, the process following the arrest of a juvenile is the same. The person, let's call him Fred, is ordered to appear in Juvenile Court (some states call it Family Court). There Fred goes through a procedure called intake, where he is seen by an officer of the court, usually a probation officer.

In first offenses or minor offenses, the process could end there. After screening, the case could be adjusted (dismissed).

If the case continues, a statement of charges is prepared and turned over to the legal department for prosecution.

If Fred is facing serious charges, he could be detained for the next three days until he appears before a judge for a judicial hearing. No jury is present. The purpose of that hearing is to determine "probable cause": Is there sufficient evidence to believe Fred did what he is charged with?

If the judge finds there is probable cause, the next step is a fact-finding hearing. This hearing is similar to a trial for an adult, except that it, too, is held only before a judge.

If Fred is judged guilty at the fact-finding hearing, a dispositional hearing is scheduled about eight weeks later.

At this third hearing, which is like the sentencing phase of an adult trial, the judge determines whether Fred is placed on probation, given a conditional discharge, or sent to a special institution for juveniles.

That is how it works today, but it hasn't always been that way.

For centuries, young criminals were treated like adults. In Europe, even as late as the 19th century, children as young as ten and eleven were hanged alongside adult criminals for robbery and other offenses. In America, juveniles were tried as adults and sent to regular prisons.

At the turn of the 20th century, a reform movement called for different treatment of juveniles. The goal was to help troubled children rather than punish them. There were some tradeoffs in that reform, however. In return for special consideration from the court, juveniles gave up certain rights of due process, primarily the right to counsel. They had to rely on the fairness, discretion, and good intentions of the juvenile court.

"The ideal would be to have judges who are capable of meeting standards in all those areas. But we seldom meet the ideal," says Professor Haley. "Not only that, too many judges are inexperienced in juvenile cases."

An example of the result of that kind of inexperience is what happened to Gerald Gault in an Arizona court in June 1964 after he and another boy were arrested for making an obscene phone call.

Two hearings were held before a judge. The only people present at the hearings were Gerald, his parents, the judge, and two probation officers. The proceedings were informal. No transcript was made, and no one was sworn to testify. The woman who filed the complaint was not even present.

Gerald was on probation because of an incident six months earlier when he was with another boy who had stolen a women's purse. At the current hearing, the probation officers gave the judge a "referral report," but

Gerald's parents were not informed what was in the report.

At the end of the second hearing, the judge sentenced Gerald to serve at the state industrial school until he turned twenty-one. He was fifteen at the time. Had Gerald been an adult, the maximum punishment for that crime would have been a fine of $50 or imprisonment for not more than two months.

Because of the obvious injustice of the decision, Gerald's parents retained lawyers to appeal the case. The appeal was based on the legal concept *parens patriae*, which permits the court to intervene to protect the welfare of a child.

Arguing that this concept should not be substituted for due process and constitutional rights, the attorneys took the case to the U.S. Supreme Court. On May 15, 1967, the court ruled that a child in a delinquency hearing must be given certain rights, including notice of charges, right to counsel, right to confront and cross-examine witnesses, and protection against self-incrimination.

That decision had the potential for solving some major problems within the system, but in many ways it made matters more difficult. In numerous cases, serious offenders have slipped through on a technicality of the law. Thus, some experts believe we have gone too far in protecting the rights of offenders.

WHY DO WE HAVE PUNISHMENT?

The primary reason for punishing criminals is to establish a sense of fairness and justice, to create order, and to assure law-abiding citizens that criminals will not get away with it.

Punishment was also long considered the best deterrent to crime. If criminals were quickly and severely punished, they and others would think twice about breaking the law.

That sounds logical. Unfortunately, it doesn't always work. The truth of the matter is that most criminals act out of habit, rather than rational thought. Another truth is that more criminals come out of our penal system than go into it. These truths have been recognized since the early 1900s by criminologists and sociologists.

In his 1938 book *Crime and the Community*, Frank Tannenbaum wrote that criminals do not think about the consequences of their actions; therefore, the concept of punishment has little effect on them. "Punishment does not reform. It does not alter the criminal who is already formed, nor does it act as a deterrent upon others who are thrown in the way of crime by the subtle incidence of companionship, habit, appetite, judgment, and opportunity."

Not much has changed since then. The inability of our prisons to rehabilitate and reform criminals is proved by the very fact that so many of them are repeat offenders.

Does Punishment Work?

The purpose of punishment is to convince a person that he or she should not repeat an action. A mother spanks her child for running into the street, hoping that he will remember it the next time he considers stepping off the curb. Sometimes the threat of punishment is enough. "If you break curfew one more time, I'm taking the car keys away for a month."

The penal system is much more complicated, but it is based on the same premise. Sometimes it works, and sometimes it doesn't.

It is very difficult to measure the effectiveness of punishment as a deterrent to crime. Even extensive studies have produced no numbers that clearly say yes or no. A well-known criminologist, Linda Anderson, came to the conclusion that ". . . there is not yet any clear or cohesive support for deterrence."

In *At a Tender Age*, Rita Kramer offers the opinion that punishment or the threat of it may work better for juveniles than for adults. She cites the Chicago Unified Delinquency Intervention Services project of the mid-1970s. One part of that study focused on juveniles who were placed in community homes, where they received counseling. If they failed to turn their life around, the next step was training school. The other part of the study concerned juveniles who had already been sentenced to the training school.

The study concluded, "An awareness of the possibility of being sent to a locked institution has a deterrent effect both on those who have experienced it and those who have heard about it from others."

The problem with the system is that not enough kids are caught and punished. There are as many loopholes for kids as for adults, and many criminals, young and old, actually commit twelve crimes for every one they are arrested for.

If We Didn't Need Punishment

Charles Silberman says, "Acceptance of the legitimacy of law is a far more effective instrument of social control than is fear of punishment."

That "legitimacy" has to do with authority and respect for authority, with willingness to obey the law because it is the law. Do you come home from a date on time because you respect your parents and don't want to lose their trust? Or because you're afraid of being grounded?

Most of us operate out of fear of punishment, but we would be better persons if we worked from the other angle. If the only thing that kept us from doing something wrong was fear of punishment, we'd simply find better ways of doing it. We wouldn't really be law-abiding citizens—just clever citizens.

It is far more beneficial to take control of our own lives. We do not steal from other kids at school because that is wrong. We do not lie to our parents because that is wrong. We do not cheat on tests because that is wrong.

Making productive decisions instead of destructive ones builds our confidence and self-esteem. It also can pave the way for significant changes in behavior. This approach can work for something as minor as breaking a bad habit and as major as rehabilitation of hardened criminals.

It works at a place called Delancy Street.

An article in *PARADE* magazine (March 15, 1992) described Delancy Street and what it did for Robert, who had lived on the streets of San Francisco from the age of ten.

Through his teen years, Robert supported himself by hustling and selling drugs; he was arrested twenty-seven times for armed robbery. At age nineteen, Robert was sent to the federal penitentiary at San Quentin, California, and he admitted that he wanted to go there. "I had no belief in myself," he said. "No hope. No trust in nothing or nobody. The reason I wanted to go to prison was because that's where I could be somebody. But when I got there, nothing in prison excited me, because I'd done everything by then."

Robert turned his life around when he went to Delancy Street in 1987. The organization was founded by Dr. Mimi

Silbert, a criminologist, and it has some unique characteristics. It operates on a system of total self-sufficiency. All residents work to support the group. They follow strict rules of behavior and self-government. Each resident must develop at least three marketable skills and earn a high school equivalency diploma.

The Delancy Street Foundation operates several businesses that provide jobs for the residents. It also built a complex containing 177 apartments, meeting rooms, a movie theater, a swimming pool, and space for some of its businesses.

Dr. Silbert patterned Delancy Street after her own experience in Boston. "Delancy Street functions the way my own family did. I've duplicated here what worked for me in that neighborhood where everybody looked out for everybody else as we struggled upward. It was like holding hands while climbing a mountain. Together we rise or together we fall. And that's what happens here every day."

New arrivals at Delancy Street start at the bottom of a long, intricate chain of command that includes every resident. A drug addict starts with sweeping floors. He is told, "Now you're no longer an addict. Why? Because we don't allow drugs here. So the question for you is how you're going to live your life without drugs."

Silbert refers to it as an "outside-in" approach. If you start acting and looking different, you will eventually change. The residents of Delancy Street have to cut their hair and wear suits. "We ask them to act as if they were upstanding citizens or successful executives, even though they feel the opposite," Silbert said. "Through external imitation, something gets internalized."

Delancy Street has had outstanding success since its founding in 1972. Despite the wide range of violent criminals who walk through the door, it has never had a violent incident. Eighty percent of the residents have kept their promise to stay at least two years, and graduates have gone on to become attorneys, business people, and skilled workers.

The key to its success is that the program gives the residents hope, responsibility, opportunities for personal success, and a sense of community spirit. Dr. Silbert tells the residents that if they are "too angry or too guilty or too hopeless to make an effort for themselves, to do it for the other guy. Because he's counting on you."

It is becoming increasingly obvious to people who work in the criminal justice system that we need more alternatives like Delancy Street. Prison is not doing it. "I interned as a prison psychologist," says Dr. Silbert, "and it was clear to me that this system of punishment doesn't work. The people who wind up there are given everything, all paid for by the taxpayers, and they are responsible for nothing. And then we wonder why, when they come out, they're no different."

Other programs are taking a similar approach to rehabilitation. We'll look at some of them in Chapter 13.

CHAPTER 11

Speaking Out

"**N**o one knows for sure when they will be a victim of violence. It could be innocent you who always minds your business. Bullets have no name nor eyes. That's why there is no strategy for surviving in a violent world. You can protect yourself as best as you possibly can, but when the time comes for you to be hit with violence, you won't be missed."

The quotation is from one of a series of essays written by teenagers for Dr. Deborah Prothrow-Stith. For her book *Deadly Consequences*, she asked a Boston high school class to write about their thoughts and feelings on the problem of violence.

Many of the kids had firsthand experience with serious violence, and their concerns were very real. But as the violence grows, teens from other backgrounds and circumstances have similar concerns.

A group of high school students—sophomores, juniors, and seniors—discussed the problem from their viewpoint. They live and attend school in Plano, Texas, a suburb of Dallas, and their experience with violence is more limited than that of the teens in Boston. However, the problem is very much on their minds.

Only two of the boys had had direct experience with violence. Barry told of an incident when another boy kept taunting him to fight in the halls at school. Barry tried to avoid a confrontation, but one day the boy boxed him in at the end of a hallway.

"It didn't seem like I could avoid it," Barry said. "So we fought. I beat him up, and I thought that would be the end of it. But it wasn't. He followed me home from school and beat me up.

"We could have gone on like that forever. I could have beat him up again. Then he'd beat me up. I guess that's what some people do, and that's why it never stops."

What Barry did was tell his father about the incident, and he called the police. A complaint was filed, and the other boy never bothered Barry again. "I don't know what they did to him," Barry said. "We never went to court or anything, but he left me alone."

Barry realized that it is not always so simple. Using the system doesn't always work, but he still thought we should try. "That's what it's there for," he said. "And more people should use it instead of trying to take care of it themselves."

All the teens agreed that lack of parental control and discipline is one of the causes of violence. Tony told of his experiences as an example.

"We have these guys in our neighborhood who are home alone a lot. Their parents go out of town or work late and the guys are by themselves. They run around the neighborhood destroying people's property. Shooting lights out with BB guns and stuff like that.

"I hate to go out sometimes because I know they'll be there. They pick on anybody who is around and try to scare us with threats and stuff. The only time I go out is when I know their parents are home."

Tony said if those boys weren't so mean, he'd feel a little sorry for them. "Even when the parents are home, they neglect those kids. The mother is always sending them outside. And the father doesn't spend much time with them. Neither one of the parents will do anything to punish the boys when they get in trouble.

"One time they were throwing fireworks into our pool, so my dad went over to tell their father. He didn't get upset or anything. He just told Dad, 'Oh, well, boys will be boys.' I thought Dad was going to lose it right there."

Jason also thought too many kids are left alone too much. "It seems like nobody cares about family life anymore. There's no guidance. Parents need to teach their kids, especially when they are thirteen and fourteen. That's when kids are trying to figure out who they are, and they need parents to help them."

Ryma agreed that kids need guidance from their parents, but she also thinks kids alone are missing something else. "Kids miss the closeness and love of a family," she said. "They don't get the attention they need, then they have to get bad attention."

Barry mentioned that kids don't get to learn by example when the parents are not involved with them. "My dad doesn't condone fighting. He tells me there are better ways to work it out. I know some kids whose fathers tell them to 'duke it out,' without realizing the kid could be in danger. I don't always listen to Dad, but I know he's right, and I've seen him find alternatives to fighting to work out a disagreement."

Barry thought that the kids who have no one to tell

them or show them any different don't know how to find an alternative. "It's a kind of ignorance, and once they're boxed into it [fighting], they can't find another way out."

The group also talked about punishment and the fact that the law doesn't seem able to do much. "No one's afraid of the law," Jerry said. "You can be out in six months and doing it all over again."

Jerry's solution, suggested half in jest and half seriously, was chain gangs. "Breaking rocks is very unappealing work," he said with a grin. "After doing that for a year, they wouldn't want to do it again."

Danielle proposed a more moderate approach. She agreed that harsh physical discipline was good, but she also thought troubled teens needed mental discipline and motivation. She suggested a program like military boot camp.

Jason agreed with the boot camp idea. "Just sticking them in prison isn't going to do anything," he said. "Give them something to do that will help them better themselves."

"Yeah," Danielle said, "crime is the easy way out. Boot camp teaches them to be responsible for others. When they live up to that responsibility, it makes them feel better about themselves. They can see some success in their life."

The group recognized that a lack of self-esteem is a primary cause of a lot of teen problems. Most kids who do drugs or are involved with violence think nobody cares about them. If no one cares, they must not be worth much.

To turn kids around from a life of violence and crime, Jerry agreed that the boot camp idea was better than the chain gang. "Boot camp would help with self-esteem. By the time you finish with boot camp, you feel like you're part of the team. You matter."

"It also teaches them discipline and gives them an opportunity for an education," Barry added.

Ryma proposed attacking the self-esteem problem before someone gets in trouble. "We need self-esteem classes in school. They [the schools] should be teaching more than facts and technology. This is especially important for kids who are missing it at home. They need to have someone who cares. If they learn to be happy with themselves, they don't have to search out other means."

These teens attend a school that has no metal detectors. In fact, they said that most of the adults don't think there's a problem with weapons at school. "There are guns around here, though," Keith said. "One day a friend of mine pushed a kid's gym bag off a bench; it fell open and he could see a .45 in it. Lots of kids have guns in their cars, too. But they're just as afraid of getting caught with them as we are of them having them."

Considering the possibility that their school could have metal detectors in the future, the teens thought they could deal with it. They even thought it would be okay to have to go through the searches other students already experience.

"I'd feel uncomfortable if I had to go through searches," Ryma said. "But if it protects one life, it would be worth it."

Jason thought people shouldn't rely on metal detectors because there are ways to get around them. Jerry agreed, and gave an example.

"I read in the paper about this incident that happened up north, New Jersey, I think. One day this principal didn't turn on the metal detectors because the mayor was coming to the school. I guess he thought it would be insulting to have the mayor walk through a metal detector. So while the detectors were off, a kid brought a gun to school and shot someone."

These teens have friends who attend schools with detectors, so they realize that it can create a prisonlike atmosphere. But they didn't think it had to become a negative factor for learning. "It's up to everyone's own attitude," Jerry said. "If you really want to learn, you can. You just have to turn your attitude around. Don't look at it as a negative."

All the students believed that some sort of gun control is a necessity if we are ever to stop the deaths by violence. Ryma commented, "Without guns, it would be harder for people to kill each other. A drive-by shooting is a lot easier than a drive-by stabbing."

Danielle called the escalation in gun possession "our own little arms race. The criminals get more guns, so the police have to get more. Then more people need guns to protect themselves. It goes on and on."

Several suggestions were made for gun control: a waiting period before being able to buy a gun, stricter rules of ownership, and classes in gun safety. Jerry proposed teaching gun safety in school. "Maybe they should require a semester on riflery the way they do health," he said. "Or at least offer a course in marksmanship and safety."

Tony agreed that might be a good idea. "Everybody looks at a gun or rifle as a means to hurt someone. They don't see it as a sport or protection. If you made it a sport, everyone would have to master gun safety. They'd have to maintain certain standards or they'd lose their privileges."

The question of the constitutional right to keep and bear arms came up, but most of the teens thought it was outdated. "Back when it was written, people needed it," Keith said. "Now we don't."

"Nowadays having a gun is for protection or to get the other guy first," Ryma added. "If there was a way to get rid of all the guns, it would be better. We don't need them. Some people are responsible about guns, but others aren't. They buy a gun for protection and they don't know anything about it. Most of the time they end up getting shot with their own gun."

"Do we need to bear arms anymore?" Tony asked. "Who are we fighting? Each other? It was meant to protect ourselves from our enemies, not our neighbors."

In regard to violence in entertainment, specifically films and television, most of the teens had similar opinions. Barry thought young children should not see a lot of violence. "As you get older you can discern between fantasy and reality," he said. "Little kids can't."

But what about older kids who can't make that distinction? Lots of kids don't have the ability to reason things out that completely.

Barry hadn't thought of that, so he was willing to concede that perhaps too much violence isn't good for anyone.

The group agreed that the extreme violence is unnecessary, and Jerry even got brave and said why not have more films with no violence. "Movies don't make you think anymore," he said. "Most of the movies are just 'sit and watch.' We need more films like 'Driving Miss Daisy.' Something that makes a good point."

That comment opened a discussion about what films they go to and why. Most of the teens had seen the recent violent films but didn't think about the excessive violence. Tony said he gets interested in the special effects and doesn't think much about the rest of the film.

Tony also mentioned the peer pressure to go to those films. "If your parents tell you you can't see anything but

PG films, you're out of the crowd," he said. "You go to school and everyone's talking about all the other films. They make fun of you if you say you didn't see it."

Derrick said he didn't go to many violent films, partly by choice and partly because of his parents. But he didn't think we should completely whitewash films. "You need to understand about reality," he said. "You don't have to experience it, but if you're never exposed, you grow up naive."

Ryma thought that the way people are portrayed in movies is just as bad as the violence. "They need to have better role models in film," she said. "Even the good guys look like bad guys. The renegade cop and characters like that."

"Toymakers and toys have a lot to do with it, too," Keith said. "GI Joe used to be my idol. Then when I got a little older I didn't want it anymore. But some kids grow up thinking they've got to be just like those action heroes."

Despite wrong messages being promoted through entertainment, the group didn't think much could be done about it. "It's so hard to censor," Barry said. "There are too many self-interest groups out there. And we do live in a free country with a free enterprise system."

Ryma made a final comment about the need for finding alternatives to violence to solve problems. "There's nothing that bad that you should kill over. People need to talk about things. If something's going on bad at home or at school, use the system to solve the problem."

The discussion ended with the shared hope that good sense would eventually win out. We can't continue as we are, so the alternative is to find ways to eliminate the causes of violence.

This might be a good time for you to think about your

opinions on these topics. Maybe you'd like to get a few friends together and talk about it as these teens did. Who knows, you might come up with some pretty good alternatives.

CHAPTER 12

Anatomy of an Argument

The whole idea of not fighting, not standing up for ourselves, is quite alien to most people. If we don't do it, people will take advantage of us. We will become victims. We have to protect ourselves.

But, as we have seen in earlier chapters, satisfying that need for protection has only added fuel to the problem of violence. Gary Cooper of the Dallas Peace Center sums it up this way, "If you choose to base your decisions on the threat of violence, then that's what your life is about. Even if you never fight anybody or shoot anybody, you're preparing all the time. That has to do something to people. That has to change them."

Cooper made that comment to newspaper reporters a few days after he had been savagely beaten by two robbers outside the Center in March 1991.

After spending several years studying nonviolence, passive resistance, and other pacifist philosophies, Cooper started working at the Peace Center, editing its newsletter. His decision to become active in promoting peace was based on a concern for the future. "That's the only way I think the world can survive."

Some people thought the attack might change Cooper's attitudes. He was left with a broken jaw, among other injuries, and he had all the natural reactions of anger and frustration. But he was surprised that anyone thought it would change his belief in pacifism. He believes the men who beat and robbed him should be arrested and put away, but he doesn't think revenge or retaliation is a solution. Not because he's soft, or a wimp, but because it doesn't work in the long run. "I don't oppose violence because I'm some sweet, gentle person who couldn't harm a fly. And it's not that I can't stand the thought of fighting," he says. "It's just that violence doesn't work. Some people say the way to get peace is to be more violent than anybody else. I think the way you get peace is you don't do violence. This society loves and depends on and breeds violence."

Gary is not alone in believing that nonviolence is the best response. In an article in *PARADE* magazine (Feb. 9, 1992), Lynn Minton interviewed several teenagers from across the nation on their opinions of fighting as a way to solve problems. Peter, a seventeen-year-old from New Mexico, said, "If a bully was picking on me, I probably would *want* to hit back. It's hard not to when you're angry." Peter has not hit back, however, because he doesn't think fighting is right. He doesn't worry if others think he's not brave. "Maybe *they* will, but I won't."

Kelly, who lives in Kentucky and is also seventeen, agreed that fighting is not the thing to do. She said she would try to talk about the problem and resolve it that way. If that didn't work, she said, she would probably just walk away. "That doesn't mean you're a coward. It just means you're smart enough to know that punching some-body is not going to fix any problems."

Because our anger response to a situation is so instan-taneous, we may think acts of violence are totally reac-tionary. Someone gets in our face, and we shove him. Someone is breaking into our car, so we jump him. We feel immediate anger, perhaps even a need for self-protection, and we react.

For the most part, we have accepted those reactions as okay, normal, permissible, even commendable, so we've done nothing to stop the chain reaction. But what if we could stop it?

In *A New Guide to Rational Living*, Albert Ellis and Robert Harper offer an interesting possibility. "Human emotions do *not* magically exist in their own right, and do *not* mysteriously flow from unconscious needs and desires. Rather, they almost always directly stem from ideas, thoughts, attitudes or beliefs, and can usually get radically changed by modifying our thinking process."

For example, think about some of the attitudes and beliefs that Tim had in Chapter 1. He believed that people in the neighborhood were a threat to him. That belief led to an attitude that to survive he had to be meaner and tougher than the next guy. The result was that a great deal of frustration and anger controlled his life for a long time. When Tim started to think more rationally about what was going on, he realized that he could change it.

Ellis and Harper believe that the more clearly a person can think during a situation, the more control he will have over his emotions and over his reactions to those emotions.

RATIONAL THOUGHT

The ability to think rationally is a good coping technique for all kinds of situations, and it has the following five characteristics:

Rational thought is based on objective fact as opposed to subjective opinion. Imagine for a moment that you have an English teacher who really doesn't like you. You feel those little vibes that tell you there's a personality conflict going on. Typically, your English grade has been lower than you think you deserve. Maybe you've tried to talk to the teacher a couple of times, but she's not responsive. So you decide to blow it off. You'll do just the bare minimum to get by and not worry about it anymore. Then you come to midterms and you bomb on the test. Your first reaction is to get mad and blame it all on the teacher. "She never liked me and now she's proved it by failing me."

That's a subjective reaction—totally based on what you think and feel.

A more objective reaction would be to let go of the frustration about the teacher and how she feels about you. Then you could see the fact that you probably failed because you didn't study. You allowed the circumstance of the teacher's not liking you to manipulate your life. And all that negative thinking hurt only you. It did nothing to the teacher.

If acted upon, rational thinking most likely will result in preserving you from death or injury. Tim might have avoided a lot of fights and problems had he been able to think clearly. He could have stopped letting his circumstances direct his actions.

If acted upon, rational thought can lead you to your personal goals more quickly. Say, for instance, you're trying out for the football team. You're not as big as some of the other guys, so it's harder for you. And the coach is always in your face, pushing you and treating you as if you're never going to be good enough. Sometimes he makes you so mad you want to scream at him to get off your back.

If you are never able to step back from the situation and look at it calmly and rationally, you may end up walking off the field in anger and frustration. On the other hand, you could recognize that, yes, you do have to work harder. And, yes, you do have to prove yourself to the coach. Those are the objective facts, and once you accept them, you can channel your energies into making the team. The alternative is to be controlled by your negative attitude and feelings and probably end up getting cut.

If acted upon, rational thought prevents undesirable conflict. Perhaps someone at school tells you that your best friend is telling lies about you. Your immediate reaction is to find your friend and confront her. "How dare you!" If you think about it for a minute, though, you realize that the girl who told you doesn't like your friend. Maybe she's even tried to cause trouble between you before. So instead of storming off to confront your friend, you can simply ask her what, if anything, she said. There's no need for conflict.

Rational thought minimizes inner conflicts and turmoil. When we are not able to step out of ourselves to view a situation, we tend to see everything in a negative light. If a teacher doesn't like me, there must be something wrong with me. If the coach yells at me all the time, I must not be good enough. That kind of negative thinking is self-defeating and creates even more turmoil. It robs us of confidence and can even set us up for failure. How often have we wondered if we'll ever be good at something? As long as we keep wondering, we may never find out.

PUTTING A LID ON IT

Finding a way to control anger is the first step toward not fighting, but anger is a tough emotion to deal with. It can overwhelm you in an instant and rise to such power that you literally don't know what to do. Some people describe feeling like an overinflated balloon that will burst at any moment.

Usually when we're angry we believe that we are totally right and the other person is wrong. (There's that "subjective opinion" again.) If we stand firm on that conviction, there is little room for a satisfactory resolution. The outcome is more apt to be like two bulls butting heads in a pasture.

Although the surge of anger is immediate, some things do go on subconsciously before we erupt. In his book *Overcoming Frustration and Anger*, P.A. Hauck outlines six steps of irrational decisions that lead most of us to anger.

1. I want something.
2. I didn't get it and I'm frustrated.
3. It's awful and terrible not to get what I want.
4. You shouldn't frustrate me! I must have my way!
5. You are bad for frustrating me.
6. Bad people ought to be punished.

Moving from number one to number six can happen very quickly, and we're probably not even aware of the process.

An example is what frequently happens when very young children fight over a toy. A group of three-year-olds are in the park. Teddy is happily playing with a truck in the sand. Jimmy decides he wants the truck and tries to take it away. Teddy won't let go, and Jimmy falls back in the sand, frustrated and angry. He picks up a plastic baseball bat and whops Teddy on the head.

In the normal course of growing up, we come to realize there are better ways of getting what we want. Maturity and reason help us learn to control our reactions to those feelings of frustration.

We still want things. We still feel frustrated when something or someone stands in our way. We learn, however, not to bash our opponent over the head.

Dr. Prothrow-Stith believes that these lessons are best taught at home. Parents are best positioned to teach a child how to manage anger and aggression nonviolently. "Kids need to grow up seeing people control their anger," she writes. "They need to learn that anger is not too dangerous or too overwhelming to face, to feel, and to let go of. If they don't have any real-life role models they can look up to, how are they ever going to counter the messages that are thrown at them from every direction? Film, television, and the success of every street gang in America tell young people that violence is the only outlet for anger."

Dr. Prothrow-Stith also believes that if parents are not teaching their kids how to control anger, someone should intervene. She has worked extensively in the public health field, and she suggests that doctors should react the same way to threats of violence as they do to threats of suicide. She writes of a seventeen-year-old boy she stitched up one night in the emergency room in Boston. He had been in a fight, and she could still see barely controlled anger in him. When she explained that she was an intern just learning how to do sutures, he told her she would get lots of practice; he was going to go out and fight the guy who cut him, then she could stitch him up, too. Several years later, she remembered the incident when she was researching her book, and she realized that there is no provision for doctors to take action in cases of violence and anger. She believes there should be. The boy's threat of violence was no less dangerous than had he threatened to go home and take a bunch of pills. In fact, it could have been more dangerous.

She recommends that the Public Health Service take an active role in teaching people how to deal with anger. Schools could also develop classes to help young people learn to find alternatives to violent expression of their anger.

Some techniques for controlling compulsive aggressive behavior are already being used in counseling chronic abusers. R.W. Novaco, a psychologist with extensive experience in treating abusers, encourages clients to use a method called "self-talk" to remain calm in stressful situations. In therapy sessions, Novaco encourages them to practice talking themselves through a situation as a rehearsal for the real thing.

Talking to yourself may seem a little weird, but it can help you to keep more control. It keeps you consciously connected to reason so your mind doesn't go through the automatic sequence of anger.

Novaco suggests that we all practice what we would do before situations arise. Create a provoking incident in your mind, and then rehearse what you could say to yourself to keep from reacting.

"This may be rough, but I can handle it. I don't have to lose control. I can stay cool. I don't have to take this personally."

Using the technique of self-talk, you strive for four main objectives:

1. Keep the situation in proportion. "I know how to deal with it."
2. Relax. "I can stay cool."
3. Believe in your ability for control. "I can handle this."
4. Focus on the problem. "I don't have to take this personally."

In moving from anger to violence, Jeanne P. Deschner believes we go through several stages at which we could make a choice to stop the progression. She outlines it this way in *The Hitting Habit*:

Start—Pain or frustration occurs.
Choice point 2—Fear is added.
Choice point 3—Evil intent is assumed.
Choice point 4—Judgment is passed.
Choice point 5—Retaliation begins.
Arrival at primitive rage—Violence seems good and necessary.

Addressing each of the stages in order, Deschner offers suggestions for stopping the sequence.

At the **start**, the easiest way to stop a conflict is not letting it get started. Deschner also encourages "self-talk": "Is this worth a fight? Will I gain anything by fighting?"

At choice point 2, **don't add the fear**. Maybe the other guy will back off and leave me alone if I stay cool. If I show that I'm afraid, he may think he has to prove something.

At choice point 3, **don't assume evil intent**. Maybe something is going on that I can't see yet. Perhaps something happened to trigger his anger that has nothing to do with me.

At choice point 4, **don't pass judgment**. He made a mistake. Maybe I did, too. We're both human. Maybe we can work this out.

At choice point 5, **don't begin retaliation**. Maybe we should talk some more. If it was just a misunderstanding, no one's to blame. Maybe we can find a way to resolve the problem.

All this is helpful in understanding our behavior and some of the things that influence us, but it is still up to each of us individually to do the right thing. We can have programs, and counseling, and education, but it all comes down to the choices each of us makes.

Psychologist Rollo May suggests that we should all strive for innocence—not the childish, blind innocence that closes our eyes to danger, but an innocence that approaches life with freshness and purity.

You're probably saying, "Right. I can do that. And get laughed right out of school." But consider the possibilities.

Great leaders with nonviolent philosophies were people with a healthy innocence. People like Gandhi and Martin Luther King regarded life with awe and respect. It was that attitude that guided their movements. The "authentic innocence" of a nonviolent person is the source of his power. It does not block awareness, nor does it exclude responsibility.

Innocence does not avoid evil, but confronts it. We can sit back and say we have no connection to the violence around us, but we are all part of the tragic events that occur in society. That does not mean we have to beat ourselves up about it.

It just means we have to increase our ethical sensitivity to injustice and perhaps act against it when necessary.

CHAPTER 13

Fighting Violence

Some people hold that stricter adherence to "law and order" is all we need to solve the problems of violence. History has shown, however, that it is not so simple. Law is designed to uphold the "order" of society, and too often "order" is merely acceptance of the status quo.

(Today, we "accept" that gangs rule many of our neighborhoods and schools.) We "accept" that more people should have guns to protect themselves. We "accept" the influences of life-style and entertainment that promote violence.

Professor Haley believes we will begin to stem the tide of violence when it becomes bad enough to touch a majority of the people's lives. Then people will step forward and take some sort of action.

That is already happening in neighborhoods across the country. People are coming out of their houses and apartments and telling the dope dealers and gang members to clear out. In effect, they're saying, "This is our home, our street, and we don't want you here. We want to live in safety, not fear."

Neighborhood Crime Watch groups have become common in recent years, and police departments welcome them. As the crime rate escalates, the police rely more and more on citizens who take some responsibility for crime prevention.

Richard Neely, Chief Justice of the West Virginia Supreme Court, believes these groups will continue to play an important role in crime and violence prevention. In *Take Back Your Neighborhood*, he offers some guidelines.

He suggests that anticrime patrols adopt rules similar to those that govern the Guardian Angels. That organization, which originated in New York, now operates in several major cities, patrolling high-crime areas. Their rules require that members:

- Be no younger than sixteen.
- Have no criminal record.
- Commit to a regular schedule and be dependable.
- Receive training through crime prevention programs at the police department.
- Know the laws of citizen's arrest and reasonable force.

Neely suggests that patrols wear some kind of uniform to establish unity and authority. He stresses that they should be unarmed. "They don't have to carry guns to be effective. In fact, if they carry guns it will probably lead to more violence."

Neely cites two successful examples of patrols.

The Block Watch program in Seattle has lowered the crime rate between 48 and 61 percent. Started in 1975 with 100 blocks participating, it had grown to 2,800 blocks in 1990. Residents patrol their blocks daily and report any suspicious activity to the police, making it more difficult for criminals to operate on those streets.

In Houston, civilians patrol an area between burned-out nightclubs and a few well-maintained homes. By sheer presence and numbers, they manage to keep hookers and dealers on their side of the street.

All without guns or violence.

Groups need not be as formally organized as Neely suggests to be effective. The Neighborhood Watch program that is common in cities across the nation concentrates on four areas of crime prevention: self-protection, burglary protection, property identification, and crime reporting. The participants do not necessarily patrol the streets, although some do.

Detroit has a highly successful Neighborhood Watch program in an area called Crary-St. Mary's. The police crime prevention unit educated residents as to what constitutes suspicious activity, how to give an accurate description, and how to practice personal safety.

In *Fighting Violent Crime in America*, Ronald S. Lauder writes, ". . . robberies in that area of Detroit dropped 56 percent compared to a drop of 17 percent in a similar area only beginning to organize neighborhood watches. Housebreakings were down 61 percent compared to 13 percent; larcenies from autos fell 51 percent compared with 5 percent in the other area."

Lauder describes the operation of a number of Neighborhood Watch groups, all with similar rates of success. Perhaps a resident of Belleville, New Jersey, says it all, "This place is getting to be the kind of neighborhood it was twenty years ago when you could leave a bicycle outside and nobody would touch it. And that's the way we want it."

I'M KING OF THE CASTLE

Rollo May believes that violence is only a symptom. The disease might be powerlessness, insignificance, or injustice. May combines all three into the term **impotence**. It is that impotence we have to deal with to strike the disease at its core. "We must find ways of sharing and distributing power so that every person . . . can feel that he, too, counts, that he, too, makes a difference . . . and is not cast out on the dunghill of indifference as a nonperson."

Most of us have grown up assuming that having power means being on top, king of the castle. It implies a distinction between "superior" and "inferior," with the power belonging to the "superior."

According to John W. Gardner, former Secretary of Health, Education, and Welfare, that distinction defines a misuse of power. In his book *On Leadership*, Gardner defines power as "the capacity to ensure the outcomes one wishes and to prevent those one does not wish."

Some people have power as a result of position in life. Parents, teachers, police officers, executives, and politicians all have power within their sphere of influence. Other people have power without position. Their power comes from qualities of persuasiveness, leadership, or charisma.

Power can be broken down into the following categories:

Exploitive—the most destructive type of power. It involves use of people for the benefit of the person holding the power. Slavery is the best example.

Manipulative—power **over** someone. People who have this kind of power manipulate others emotionally, as in managers who control their workers through threats and intimidation.

Competitive—power **against** another. In sports, it can be used to win games, and as long as the play is fair, the power is not negative. When players resort to unfair tactics because they can't stand the thought of losing, it becomes power misused.

Nutrient—power **for** others. It is seen in people who care for others, mothers and nurses being the most common examples.

Integrative—power **with** the other. My power helps my neighbor. This is the kind of power Mother Teresa has. One does not think of her as a great leader, but considering what she has accomplished, we have to recognize her power of leadership.

All people possess the ability to develop those kinds of power. In fact, most of us have the first three pretty well nailed down. We've bossed our little brother around; we've manipulated our friends; we've committed a few fouls on the playing field.

Finding the right balance of power must be the goal. We don't want to use other people to get what we want. We don't want to destroy our relationships by being manipulative and playing mind games with our friends. And finally, we want to be honorable in our dealings with others, whether on the soccer field or in our career.

For each of us to find our own balance of power, Rollo May says we go through three levels.

Power to Be. This power starts in infancy. A baby cries, demanding that his needs be met. In that sense, he is **able to survive**. The power to be is the beginning of confidence. To be emotionally healthy, we must all feel **able to survive**.

Children who grow up without their needs being met feel **unable**. They are unsure of themselves and often overanxious in situations we might take in stride. The feeling of being **unable** can be eased with counseling. If not corrected, however, it can cause severe lifelong emotional problems.

Self-Affirmation. Each person has the need not only to be, but to **affirm** his or her own being. As we grow toward adulthood, our main concern is no longer just to survive, but to survive with some esteem. We need to feel that we are worthwhile and important to the world around us.

Usually we gain self-esteem through the love and support of family. By the time we reach young adulthood, we feel important, we have significance. If that esteem is not developed in the early years, we search for it the rest of our lives.

Self-Assertion. People who are self-assertive are saying in a way, "Here I am. I demand that you notice me." It is another way of affirming our goodness and worthiness. We want to hear from others that they notice us and are proud of us. We want our parents to come to our football games and the school play. We want our teachers to notice the extra effort we put into our research paper.

Such moments of recognition bolster our confidence. Then we begin to trust our own perceptions of our goodness and worthiness without needing constant reinforcement. That is a level of personal power that makes us much more effective in life.

THE ROOT OF THE PROBLEM

Now we can see how important it is for people to have someone who cares for them and will listen to them. It gives them the conviction that they count, they matter to someone else, they have significance. It **empowers** them.

Psychologists, sociologists, and criminologists have come

to realize that that is a critical need. If we can devise better ways of meeting that need in people who have become violent, it may be the best way of stemming the problem.

A program that uses that approach is the California Conservation Corps, started by then Governor Jerry Brown in 1976. Young people who enter the program work hard fighting forest fires and floods and building parks.

The program utilizes discipline and hard work to give the young people a sense of accomplishment. It also encourages citizenship and education. Classes are available in the evenings for those who want to finish high school or earn a GED.

The supervisors in CCC believe that the teamwork has the greatest influence on the troubled youths who come into the program. Learning to cooperate with their peers toward a common objective, often in the face of danger, fosters self-esteem and a feeling of belonging.

Forty thousand young people have successfully passed through the CCC program. Twelve other states and dozens of cities and counties have established similar programs.

Lincoln Hall, a residential treatment facility for delinquents in Westchester County, New York, also has a program that addresses the heart of the problem. It is affiliated with the Archdiocese of New York, and a number of staff members are Catholic priests.

Most of the residents are chronic truants or have been convicted of petty robbery, but they are not considered dangerous. One aim of the program is to turn them around *before* they become violent offenders.

Rita Kramer writes about Lincoln Hall in *At a Tender Age*: ". . . if effort, intentions, and atmosphere can make a difference, the people at Lincoln Hall have a shot at it."

At the facility, which resembles a resort, the boys are

cared for physically and emotionally by staff doctors. They have opportunities for swimming and other recreation designed to help them feel good about themselves.

"They've never experienced the feeling of success," said a staff member. "They think of themselves as born losers or as Mr. Con. What they have a chance to experience here for the first time is a positive attitude about themselves. The born loser can learn what it feels like to do well, the con man learns something about rules and responsibility."

A program at a Catholic camp in Tyler, Texas, is also trying to get to young people before they get into serious trouble. Called "Journey," the three-day program stresses leadership, goal-setting, self-esteem, and self-discipline. It is offered to kids in their early teens who live in gang-dominated neighborhoods and are most susceptible to gang influence.

Journey camps are held once a month. Each day, some time is spent enjoying the "great outdoors," an experience many of the boys have never had. There are also planned activities for all campers.

Under the rules, the campers live in cabins with rival gang members. "Things have become a little tense on occasion," said Bonnie Castellaw, Executive Director of The Pines, which hosts Journey. "But here they have an opportunity to work things out without guns."

Trained "coaches" serve as mentors, guides, and role models for the kids. Some of the coaches are former gang members, who can relate to the kids in a way others can't.

Seminars offer the kids a glimpse of what could be in store for them if they move into a life of violence and crime. Inmates from nearby prisons talk candidly about their experiences before and during prison, and encourage the kids to find something better to do with their lives.

A unique aspect of Journey is the follow-up program. The coaches keep in touch with the kids after they go back to their neighborhoods. "We can't just send them back with no support at all," Castellaw said. "Once they're back in a negative environment, it's too easy to forget all the lessons they learned here at the camp."

The program is still too new to measure its effectiveness, but the staff is optimistic. They believe that if they touch just one life in each group that passes through, all the planning and effort are worth it.

Texas Key is the name of a program that has centers in Dallas, Houston, and San Antonio. It is offered as an alternative to large detention centers that operate more like prisons. Staff members at the Key centers say its programs are tailored to the individual and allow a person to succeed where other facilities have failed.

The Key fosters responsibility by giving each boy specific jobs and permitting him to earn privileges by good behavior. Because many of the boys come from unstable homes and have histories of destructive behavior, emphasis is placed on counseling. "Building self-esteem and teaching life skills are vital parts of the program," according to director Martin McLee. "The counselors teach the youths how to operate in society and how to find healthy outlets for their emotions."

Dr. Prothrow-Stith is a strong believer in these programs, which she terms "second-chance opportunities." With most experts, she believes that most "high-risk" kids are redeemable, especially when help is offered while they are still young. "Many of these kids could be saved if just one adult took an interest in them, made a commitment to them."

That is what the THRIVE Center in Oklahoma City is trying to do. In an article in *PARADE* magazine

(September 8, 1991), Michael Ryan outlines the operation of THRIVE (Truancy Habits Reduced Increasing Valuable Education). Kids who are picked up by the police for truancy are taken to the Center, where they are held until their parents come to get them.

"We only release children to their parents or to another responsible adult," says Sandy Wright, a former teacher who works at the Center. "We call the parents and explain that one of them must come here, take him back to school, and arrange for him to be readmitted."

In many cases, the parents are so uninvolved in the child's life that they do not respond. That is when the system steps in with counseling and special programs. "You can't reach everybody," said John Foley, an assistant district attorney who works at the Center. "But you have to try your best." For some kids it may be the first time someone cared enough to try.

One challenge for the future, according to Dr. Prothrow-Stith, is to teach parents how to be better parents. Because so many of the problems begin at home, perhaps the solutions lie there as well. "I believe that parent training ought to be a mandatory course in every high school in our nation," she says. "We need to teach every girl and boy how to parent, how to love and care for children, how to discipline them, and how to provide for their developmental needs."

Making Our
Schools Safe

In light of all we read and hear about guns and other weapons in classrooms, fighting in the halls, and gang fights in the parking lot, one wonders if there are any schools in America where the threat of violence is not a constant worry.

Fortunately, there are, and if you are lucky enough to be attending one, you can take pride in the efforts by all to keep it that way.

According to Dr. Prothrow-Stith, a number of factors keep some schools from being swept up in the tide of violence. ("Research shows that schools with strong principals; schools that are not too large; schools where discipline is fair, but firm; schools where teachers are imbued with high expectations for every child; schools where parents are drawn into the educational orbit, are schools where learning takes place. They are also schools that are safe.")

Dr. Prothrow-Stith stresses that the quality of education is a critical factor(Kids who succeed in school are less likely to do drugs, join gangs, or commit violent acts. "Schools can prevent violence by insuring that all children are well served academically and by teaching children to manage conflict and anger.")

We have discussed managing anger in earlier chapters, but it is interesting to note here that many schools are adopting programs to help students cope with conflict and to get along with one another peacefully. According to Dr. Prothrow-Stith, all the programs share certain ideas:

- That conflict is a normal part of human interaction.
- That when people take time to explore their prejudices, they can learn to get along with (and enjoy) people whose backgrounds are different.
- That most disputes need not have a winner and a loser; win/win is the ideal solution.
- That children and adults who learn how to be assertive can avoid becoming bullies or victims.
- That self-esteem is enhanced if children learn to build nonviolent, nonhostile relationships with their peers.

As an example of how these ideas in action have had some success, Dr. Prothrow-Stith cites the Peacemakers program of a school in New York. A quarter of the students are African-American, another quarter are Hispanic, and the rest are white. Before the Peacemaker program was started, there was a lot of racial tension; now there is much less.

The teachers were trained in conflict resolution. Then they took that training to the classroom, where they taught children as young as five and six how to stand up for themselves without triggering an angry response from their peers.

In these special classes, the students frequently talk about some conflict from their own lives, and the group discusses whether it was resolved properly or not. During one such session described by Dr. Prothrow-Stith, an African-American girl talked about an incident that had upset her. As she spoke, she became increasingly upset and ended up leaving the room in tears. A Hispanic girl jumped up and asked to go after her. "I want to give her a hug," she said.

Obviously, learning to understand also led to learning to care.

Mediating programs are also becoming effective tools in curbing racial incidents and gang fights in schools.

According to a report in the *New York Times* (December 26, 1990), San Francisco and New York were among the first cities to establish mediating programs in the early '80s. Since then, the concept has spread considerably.

In New Mexico a mediating program operates in more than 100 elementary and secondary schools, many in remote areas such as Indian reservations and small Hispanic communities. Staff trainers have also taken conflict mediation to correctional institutions for young people.

In Ann Arbor, Michigan, which has had conflict management classes for three years, all students from five to eighteen are reached. Training is also offered to staff members, including bus drivers and cafeteria workers.

In Pittsburgh, students who train to be mediators are given diplomas in a courtroom ceremony. There they swear to be fair and impartial mediators and to maintain confidentiality. The young mediators work in the schools and are also called upon to help settle community conflicts.

Teen mediators believe the system works so well because it's kids helping kids. The success has yet to be measured statistically, but the growing interest in mediation speaks volumes.

Peer counseling groups are also being established in schools. Most students prefer to talk their problems out with peers rather than adults.

One such group in Richardson, Texas, had its greatest challenge when a student committed suicide during an English class. The peer counselors work with a crisis intervention team that includes psychologists, adult counselors, the principal, and other school administrators. The team stepped in within minutes of the tragedy, and the adults were not surprised that the students talked most to the peer counselors.

TAKING BACK OUR SCHOOLS

Increasing security at the schools that have the most serious violence problems is an immediate step to be taken. Metal detectors and security patrols can reduce the number of guns and other weapons on school campuses and save lives.

That is a reality that hit New York City when two boys were shot to death in an East New York high school. Within a few days, the mayor announced a plan to upgrade security at the city's most dangerous high schools. For the boys who were killed and their parents, it was a move that came too late, but no one disagreed with the action. Even students recognized the need for security.

Most people hope that the need for high-tech security will be temporary. A more lasting solution lies somewhere in a combined effort of school administrators, teachers, parents, and students who pull together and say, "We've had enough."

The movie "Stand and Deliver" is a perfect example of how effective that approach can be. Most of the focus is on the principal for having the courage and commitment to confront the problem. Jaime Escalante arrived at Garfield High School in 1976 to find it a haven for gang members and school failures. His first move was to challenge the students to stop letting gang activity rule the school. Then he challenged them to get serious in the classroom.

The key to his approach was bolstering the kids' self-esteem and giving them something at which they could succeed. Nobody, including the students, thought they could pass advanced placement courses in math, but Escalante wouldn't let them give up. He pushed, he shouted, he threatened, and in the end the kids started believing in their own abilities.

Another factor in Escalante's success was getting the parents involved. He went to the students' homes to urge parents to take an active role in their children's education. He asked them to support the children's efforts, recognize accomplishments, and use their authority to keep the kids on track.

The effort of the students themselves cannot be overlooked. Once they started to realize personal benefits from working hard and achieving something, they took more control over themselves and others. They challenged their peers to get with the program or get out. They encouraged and assisted their friends who were struggling academically.

Garfield High School became an example of the safe school. There was strong leadership. Discipline was firm, yet fair. The teachers had high expectations of the students. And the parents were drawn into the process.

The true measure of its success, however, is not so much what happened in 1976, but the fact that it kept on happening. By the early 1990s Garfield High School had more than a dozen advanced placement courses, and 70 percent of the students went on to college.

Committed people taking action is happening in other areas of the country as well. In Utah, the Parent-Teacher Association responded to a tragedy when six young children disappeared and were later found dead. Mothers organized a "parent watch" to patrol the streets during the times when children are going to and from school. The PTA joined forces with the Utah Association of Women to designate houses where a child can go for safety. Each house is identified as a "safe house" by a poster in a front window. If a child encounters a problem, he or she can run to that house for assistance.

Mothers at a middle school in Garland, Texas, do more than patrol the streets: They patrol in the school. Their decision to take action was prompted by an incident in which a girl was pushed around by three boys. Before the incident occurred, a parent committee had already been formed to look into problems of discipline and control in the school. "Parents wanted to show that they are serious about helping maintain discipline in the school," a school district spokesman said. Teams of four mothers patrol the halls in the morning and in the afternoon, wearing badges identifying them as monitors.

The final element in stopping violence in the schools is teaching students how to resolve problems without resorting to violence.

Dr. Prothrow-Stith has developed a violence prevention

curriculum that is widely used in Massachusetts. The program, designed to provide alternatives to fighting, starts with giving the teens the cold hard facts about violence and becoming victims of violence. The next set of lessons deal with anger. In essence, the students are taught that anger is a normal emotion that they will not outgrow. It is an emotion that each of us must learn to handle without hurting ourselves or others. Reactions like waiting to cool off before confronting the person who made you angry, or getting rid of anger by punching a pillow or yelling at the sky are all healthy responses.

After recognizing the things that make them angry, the students are encouraged to find healthy ways of responding to the anger. They also list the benefits and drawbacks of fighting. "Inevitably, the list describing what is bad about fighting is longer and more impressive than the list telling what is good," says Dr. Prothrow-Stith.

Another important focus of the course is reasons not to fight. Many students find it hard to determine what is worth fighting for and what is not. With the guidance of the teacher, they act out possible scenarios in mock fights that are videotaped, analyzed, discussed, and then reworked with different endings.

The final lesson in the course is how to avoid fights. Dr. Peter Stringham, who uses the curriculum in his work in a poor white neighborhood of Boston, has his young people use a form of self-talk. He even encourages them to memorize a few responses to provocations:

"This isn't worth fighting about."

"If you've got a problem with me, I'll talk, but I don't want to fight."

"I have nothing against you and I don't want to fight."

Any discussion of not fighting always raises the question of being seen as a coward. In a society that condones violence, nonviolence is seen as "sissified" and "unmanly." Even great pacifist leaders such as Mohandas Gandhi, Martin Luther King, and Nelson Mandela have suffered ridicule and embarrassment because of their views, but they didn't let it stop them. Nor did they give in to the anger they must have felt when so many turned against them. Instead, they channeled that anger into a force to change the world.

Dr. Prothrow-Stith stresses that the violence prevention curriculum is not about being totally passive. To be passive means to take no action, and that is not what nonviolence is about.

Gandhi took a great deal of action to free India from the rule of Great Britain in 1947. Using civil disobedience, he illustrated that nonviolent resistance was a force that could achieve monumental ends.

CHAPTER 15

Joining the Fight

E ven if your life has not yet been touched by peer violence, chances are that it could be. So what can you do?

First, you can learn how not to be a victim. Take classes in self-defense and learn more about crime prevention. Make certain that the self-defense classes meet your needs and abilities. Many police organizations offer basic self-defense that does not require great strength or agility. Most martial arts, like karate or tae kwon do, are more demanding, but with practice they can be mastered by most people.

Next, you can learn to control your own anger and aggression. The violence-prevention course Dr. Prothrow-Stith developed is used in a number of states. If your school does not offer similar classes, you can take steps to get one started. Talk to your school counselor or one of your teachers. Talk to your parents. Ask members of the school board how to make a formal request to add violence prevention to the curriculum.

For more information and guidance, write to:

Violence Prevention Project
1010 Massachusetts Avenue
Boston, MA 02118

If your school does not have a mediation program, approach the people who make those decisions and let them know how beneficial it would be to your school. Information about mediation programs is available from:

School Mediation Associates
72 Chester Road
Belmont, MA 02178

SAVE (Students Against Violence Everywhere) is a national organization you might be interested in joining. It is similar to SADD (Students Against Drunk Driving) and can be established in any school. Such an organization would be helpful as a support. It is easier to do things when you know you're not the only one. For information, write to:

SAVE
West Charlotte Senior High School
2219 Senior Drive
Charlotte, NC 28216

Now comes the hard part. If you are aware of violent activity or potential violence in your school, you should report it. The risks are too great to ignore it or try to handle it yourself. Minor problems can probably be dealt with by a teacher, a counselor, or the principal. Anything more serious, especially if it is life-threatening, should be reported to school security or to the local police.

Going to the authorities may make you feel like a traitor, but consider what is at stake. If you are able to save someone's life because you had the courage to come forward, isn't that worth a little heat?

GUN SAFETY

With so many handguns in American homes today, you should know the basic rules of gun safety. The Academy of Pediatrics committee on accidents offers the following:

1. Always keep guns unloaded in the house.
2. Keep guns out of reach of small children, preferably locked up.
3. Guns should be equipped with trigger locks.
4. Ammunition should be locked up and stored away from sources of heat and electricity.
5. When handling guns in the home, be sure they are unloaded.

Training in the proper use of guns can help prevent accidents. Training is available at shooting ranges, and the NRA offers courses in gun safety and proper handling, often held at local shooting ranges.

If your parents have guns and are lax in any of those safety areas, talk to them about it. Express your concern for the family's welfare, especially if you have younger brothers or sisters. Also encourage your friends to talk to their parents who own guns.

TAKING THE PROBLEM PERSONALLY

Often the solution to a major problem begins with personal awareness and individual effort.

Although you do not yet have the accumulated knowledge and experience of adults, you are smart enough to recognize problems and probably to come up with a few solutions.

All it takes is that personal awareness and the courage to act on it—not accepting the status quo, standing up against popular belief, challenging accepted codes of behavior. Our greatest personal strength is living by a standard of high values: individual moral responsibility, caring for others, honor and integrity, tolerance, and mutual respect.

You do not have to act on a grand scale. You don't have to become a crusader, although you can if you want to. But if you just do it for yourself, it could make a difference. A great deal can be accomplished by quiet example.

A good start toward this awareness is having something to do that benefits others. Professor Haley stresses the importance of duty in our lives. "We've lost track of it somewhere along the line, and you can see the results in all levels of society. We're focused on individual rights, separate from the whole. People don't accept responsibility. Everybody's so busy taking care of themselves they don't have an awareness of how they affect the big picture."

When someone fails to accept responsibility for actions, others think that the law should somehow enforce responsibility. But Rita Kramer points out that we cannot solve every social problem by passing a law. We can't legislate responsibility, morality, honesty, and integrity.

What we can do is develop our personal code of conduct that lifts us above irresponsibility, immorality, and dishonesty. We can decide to do what is right simply because it is right. We can decide to do something to benefit others instead of ourselves. We can decide to get involved with solutions instead of becoming part of the problem.

As long as we do nothing about it, we contribute to violence.

In his book *On Leadership*, John W. Gardner writes, "If a leader holds sway by exploiting our greed or our hatreds, the evil is in us too. If a bad leader rules because of our lethargy, we are collaborators."

People to have to start standing up against all the things that are wrong in our society. One of those people could, and should, be you.

Appendix

PROTECTING YOURSELF

- Be aware of the dangers of violence all around you.
- Believe it could happen to you. Don't pretend it couldn't.
- Don't be a target. Don't look like a victim. Walk with confidence and walk quickly.
- If confronted by a mugger or a robber, throw your money in one direction and run in the other. The mugger will always choose the money over you.
- Yell "Fire" if someone attacks you. Yell it as loud and as long as you can. People respond when they hear a call of "Fire" when they wouldn't respond to a cry for help.
- In a personal attack, don't be passive. Fight back any way you can, and don't be afraid of hurting the attacker. Go for vulnerable areas such as eyes, groin, and throat, and use any weapons you can reach.
- Don't walk alone on dark streets or alleys.
- When at home alone, never open the door to a stranger.
- Learn self-defense. Make sure it's the right kind for you.
- Learn about gun safety.
- Make sure guns are locked up in your home.
- If violence breaks out at school, stay calm. Don't let yourself get pulled into the controversy. Follow orders.
- Avoid groups and activities where you know there might be drugs or weapons.

- If you hear gunshots, don't run outside to see what's going on. Call the police, then drop to the floor and stay there until the shooting stops.
- Get involved with and support safety programs at your school and in your community.
- Walk away from a challenge to fight.
- When out after dark, walk against the traffic flow and keep to well-lit main streets and populated areas if possible.
- If you are approached, head for a crowd. Don't let yourself be isolated.
- If you think you're being followed, go to the nearest house that has a light on, or go into an open place of business.
- Cross the street when nearing a rowdy crowd.
- If you are female and driving alone at night, keep doors locked and windows rolled up.
- Check inside and under your car before getting in after it has been parked.
- If followed when driving, don't go home. Drive to the nearest police station.

JUST THE FACTS

The Growing Rate of Violence

- One million people in the U.S. die each year as the result of homicide or suicide.
- In 1988-89, 2 percent of students twelve to nineteen years of age were victims of violent offenses.
- In 1992, C. Everett Koop, former Surgeon General of the U.S. Public Health Service, reported that the leading cause of death among teenage was gunshot wounds.
- Suicide is the third leading cause of death among children and teens in the U.S., a rate that has doubled in the last thirty years.
- On a national scale, arrests for homicide among juveniles went up 93 percent from 1988 to 1992.
- In Canada in 1990, 656 homicides were committed, 49 by juveniles between twelve and seventeen. A total of 269,440 crimes of violence were committed, 15,705 by juveniles.
- All documented mass murders from 1949 to 1991 in the U.S. were committed by men. Over 90 percent of all violent crime is committed by men.
- The frequency of mass murders in the U.S. has increase dramatically since 1980: from 1982 to 1986, one a year; from 1987 to 1991, two a year with the exception of 1988.
- In 1986-87, the U.S. had the highest rate of homicides by males age 15 to 24—between 4 and 73 times higher than any other industrial nation.
- Poverty, easy access to guns, and drugs are the main contributors to the rise in teen violence.

Guns and Violence

- In 1990, handguns were used in 11,750 murders in the United States. Handguns were also used in 12,000 suicides and 639,000 violent crimes.
- From 1960 to 1980 the population of the U.S. increased by 26

percent; the homicide rate due to guns increased 160 percent.

- Gunshot wounds to children age sixteen and under increased by 300 percent from 1986 to 1990.
- Of the fatalities in the 1992 Los Angeles riot, the vast majority occurred as a result of gunshot wounds.
- An estimated 200 million firearms are owned by civilians in the U.S. Handguns outsell rifles and shotguns.
- Raven Arms, a gun company in California, mass-produces cheap handguns and is the largest supplier of .25 caliber semiautomatics in the country.
- In 1991 on an average day in the U.S., 135,000 children carried a gun to school.
- Guns have replaced knives and other weapons as the weapon of choice among teems.
- Each year as many as 1,400 Americans are killed accidentally by handguns. Many of those victims are children.
- The 1989 firearms homicide rate among all fifteen- to nineteen-year-olds in metropolitan counties was nearly five times the rate in nonmetropolitan counties.
- The black teenage male firearms homicide rate in 1989 in metropolitan counties was 6.5 times the rate in nonmetropolitan counties.
- The District of Columbia had the highest firearms homicide rate for black males fifteen to nineteen, with over 250 from 1987 to 1989. Los Angeles County had the second-highest rate; Wayne County, Michigan, third.
- A study released in 1992 by the American Medical Association reported that easy access to a loaded gun may be a risk factor for accidental firearms injuries among children and may be contributing factor to adolescent suicide.
- People who won handguns for protection are more likely to keep them loaded and unlocked than people who own guns for other purposes.

- Handguns were   involved in 263 deaths in North Carolina in 1991.
- New York City had 1,500 firearms homicides in 1990.

Violence and the Media

- A 1984 study showed that kids who watch a great deal of TV violence at age eight are more likely to commit violent crimes at age thirty.
- Studies show that viewing of violence fosters the belief in children that such behavior is normal and acceptable.
- The crime of rape has increased at four times the rate of other crimes in the U.S. since 1989; the incidence of rape in films has also increased.
- A study released in 1992 by the American Medical Association found a direct correlation between television viewing and homicide in the U.S., Canada, and South Africa.

Gangs

- In 1961 in the U.S. twenty-three cities had known street gangs; in 1992 the number was 187.
- Gangs can be found in large urban areas and suburban communities with populations as small as 5,000.
- Gang members commit six times as many crimes as people of similar backgrounds who are not gang members.
- Los Angeles County has about 1,000 gangs, with a total membership of 150,000. Gang-related homicides in the county increased 200 percent between 1984 and 1991.
- From 1987 to 1991, gangs in Boston grew from six to twenty-five. From 1984 to 1988, the number of gangs in Miami grew from four to sixty.
- In 1984 most gang members were fifteen years old; in 1991, the average age was thirteen and a half.
- Most gang members come from broken or severely disturbed and deprived homes.

- Jamican gangs were linked to over 800 murders in the U.S. from 1985 to 1989.

Family-related Violence
- In 1975, between 275,000 and 750,000 children between the ages of three and seventeen were beaten by one or both parents. One in every hundred cases involves use or attempted use of guns or knives.
- Of young people in correctional institutions 72 percent said they had grown up without one or both parents.
- Teens who are deeply involved in family life rarely have problem of delinquency.
- According to a report in the *Journal of the American Medical Association*, family assaults involving firearms are twelve times more likely to result in death than assaults without weapons.

Drugs
- People who use one of the major illegal drugs commit four to six times as many crimes as nondrug users.
- The leading cause of death among teens and young adults—unintentional injuries, suicide, and homicide—are in many cases linked to drug abuse.

For Further Reading

Cain, Arthur H. *Young People and Crime*. New York: John Day Co., 1968.

Cole, George F. *The American System of Criminal Justice*. Belmont, CA: Brooks/Cole, 1989.

Deschner, Jeanne P. *The Hitting Habit*. New York: Free Press —Macmillan, 1984.

Ellis, Albert, PhD, and Harper, Robert A., PhD. *A New Guide to Rational Living*. Englewood Cliffs, NJ: Prentice-Hall, Inc., 1975.

Finckenauer, James O. *Scared Straight! and the Panacea Phenomenon*. Englewood Cliffs, NJ: Prentice-Hall, 1982.

Fromm, Erich. *The Anatomy of Human Destructiveness*. New York: Holt, Rinehart and Winston, 1973.

Gardner, John W. *On Leadership*. New York: Free Press— Macmillan, 1990.

Gelles, Richard J., and Straus, Murry A. *Intimate Violence*. New York: Simon & Shuster, 1988.

Goode, Stephen. *Violence in America*. New York: Julian Messner, 1984.

Janeway, Elizabeth. *Powers of the Weak*. New York: Alfred A. Knopf, 1980.

Juergensmeyer, Mark. *Fighting Fair; A Non-Violent Strategy for Resolving Everyday Conflicts*. San Francisco: Harper & Row, 1986.

Kramer, Rita. *In Defense of the Family*. New York: Basic Books, 1983.

———. *At a Tender Age, Violent Youth and Juvenile Justice*. New York: Henry Holt, 1988.

Landau, Elaine. *Teenage Violence*. New York: Julian Messner, 1990.

Langone, John. *Violence: Our Fastest Growing Public Health Problem*. Boston-Toronto: Little, Brown & Co., 1984.

Lauder, Ronald S. *Fighting Violent Crime in America*. New York: Dodd, Mead & Co., 1985.

Lorenz, Konrad. *On Aggression*. New York: Harcourt Brace Jovanovich, 1966.

McCuen, Gary E. *Inner-City Violence: Ideas in Conflict*. Hudson, WI: Gem Publications, 1990.

May, Rollo. *Power and Innocence: A Search for the Sources of Violence*. New York: W.W. Norton & Co., 1972.

Miller, Kent S., & Betty Davis. *To Kill and Be Killed*. Pasadena, CA: Hope Publishing House, 1989.

Prothrow-Stith, Deborah, with Michaele Weissman. *Deadly Consequences*. New York: Harper Collins Publishers, 1991.

Rohr, Janelle, ed. *Violence in America: Opposing Viewpoints*. San Diego, CA: Greenhaven Press, 1990.

Silberman, Charles E. *Criminal Violence—Criminal Justice*. New York: Random House, 1978.

Index

Acknowledgements
My special thanks to Tim and Danielle for sharing their story and their home
with me. Not only do I appreciate the fact that you trusted me enough to
open up about things that were obviously uncomfortable to talk about, but I
appreciate you kind hospitality.

Also deeply appreciated are all the other young people who shared their
stories, ideas, and opinions. It was both extremely helpful and most enjoyable
to spend time with you.

And finally, thank you to my family. One more time you came through with
the support I needed to complete this book. What would I do without you?